The Holy Roman Empire: A Very Short Introduction

VERY SHORT INTRODUCTIONS are for anyone wanting a stimulating and accessible way into a new subject. They are written by experts, and have been translated into more than 45 different languages.

The series began in 1995, and now covers a wide variety of topics in every discipline. The VSI library currently contains over 550 volumes—a Very Short Introduction to everything from Psychology and Philosophy of Science to American History and Relativity—and continues to grow in every subject area.

Very Short Introductions available now:

Available soon:

For more information visit our website

www.oup.com/vsi/

Joachim Whaley

THE HOLY ROMAN EMPIRE

A Very Short Introduction

OXFORD
UNIVERSITY PRESS

Great Clarendon Street, Oxford, OX2 6DP,
United Kingdom

Oxford University Press is a department of the University of Oxford.
It furthers the University's objective of excellence in research, scholarship,
and education by publishing worldwide. Oxford is a registered trade mark of
Oxford University Press in the UK and in certain other countries

First edition published in 2018

Impression: 1

Published in the United States of America by Oxford University Press
198 Madison Avenue, New York, NY 10016, United States of America

British Library Cataloguing in Publication Data
Data available

Library of Congress Control Number: 2018935427

ISBN 978-0-19-874876-2

Printed in Great Britain by
Ashford Colour Press Ltd, Gosport, Hampshire

Contents

Acknowledgements

I am most grateful to Andrea Keegan, Jenny Nugee, and Rebecca Darley at Oxford University Press for their support and advice during the writing and production process. Tom McKibbin was extremely helpful with the illustrations. Dorothy McCarthy and Clement Raj also provided invaluable assistance during the final stages as the manuscript turned into a book. I am also grateful to the anonymous readers of my original proposal and of my manuscript who made some valuable suggestions and pointed out some errors.

In Cambridge I am particularly grateful to the Master and Fellows of Corpus Christi College for allowing me to use the image of Otto the Great that appears as Illustration 3. Gonville and Caius College continues to provide me with a congenial place to read, think and write, as well as generous research grants.

My main reason for writing the book was to answer the questions that I have been asked by students, colleagues and friends so many times. What exactly was the Holy Roman Empire? Was it in any meaningful sense, to paraphrase Voltaire, Holy, or Roman or even an empire? I hope that this book provides answers to those questions and offers a wide-ranging introduction to the pre-modern history of the German lands.

Yet again at the end of a research project I must express my gratitude to my wife Alice, who always shows great interest in my work and puts up with me when it hits a difficult patch. She makes all the difference to everything.

Joachim Whaley

Cambridge
12 April 2018

List of illustrations

List of maps

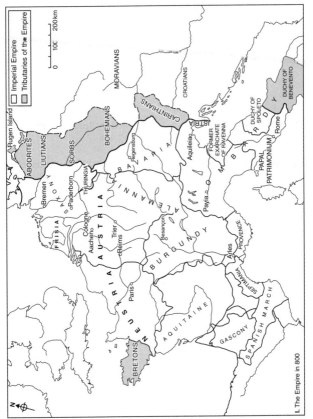

Map 1. The Holy Roman Empire, c.800.

I. The Empire in 800

Map 2. The Holy Roman Empire, 1195.

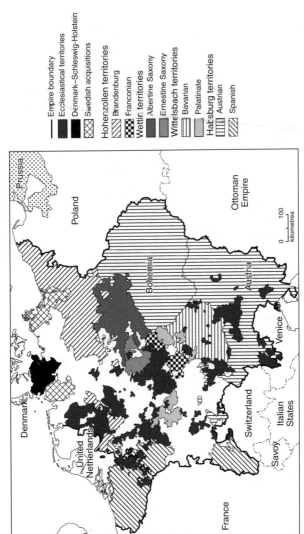

Map 3. The Holy Roman Empire, 1547.

Legend:

— Empire boundary
Ecclesiastical territories
Denmark–Schleswig-Holstein
Swedish acquisitions

Hohenzollern territories
Brandenburg
Franconian

Wettin territories
Albertine Saxony
Ernestine Saxony

Wittelsbach territories
Bavarian
Palatinate

Habsburg territories
Austrian
Spanish

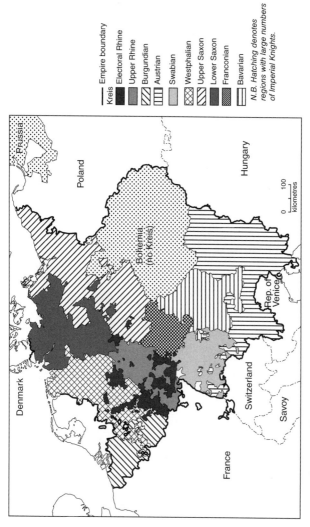

Map 4. The circles (*Kreise*) of the Holy Roman Empire, c.1648.

——	Empire boundary
	Kreis
■	Electoral Rhine
	Upper Rhine
	Burgundian
	Austrian
	Swabian
	Westphalian
	Upper Saxon
	Lower Saxon
	Franconian
	Bavarian

N.B. Hatching denotes regions with large numbers of Imperial Knights.

Prussia

Poland

Denmark

Bohemia (no Kreis)

Hungary

Rep. of Venice

France

Switzerland

Savoy

0   100

kilometres

Introduction: what was the Holy Roman Empire?

What kind of polity?

'Neither holy, nor Roman, nor an empire'—Voltaire's sardonic characterization of the Holy Roman Empire of the German Nation, recorded in his essay on the customs and spirit of nations published in 1756, has seemed to many to be a just description of a much misunderstood entity. The empire was dissolved in 1806 and by common consent it was founded in 800. Yet Charlemagne's coronation as emperor by the pope in 800 did not launch a fully fledged entity. When the German kings assumed the imperial title in 962, the empire was not yet 'holy', still less wholly 'German'. The imperial dignity established them and their successors as the premier monarchs at the head of the European table of rank until 1806. But the appellation of their realm evolved slowly until the title 'Holy Roman Empire of the German Nation' became established around 1500. The polity to which this title was attached also underwent substantial changes.

The original Frankish kingdom was essentially a tribal society which followed an elected leader. On this foundation subsequent ruling dynasties developed what became a fully fledged feudal system. At one level this continued until the empire was dissolved in 1806. The emperors and the German princes constantly performed their relationship in rituals such as the renewal of fiefdoms. Questions of rank and precedence—who should stand or sit where at key ceremonies and other formal occasions—were often the subject of bitter controversy into the 18th century. In this sense the empire remained what German historians call a 'Personenverbandsstaat' or personal association rather than a territorial state.

It was characteristic of this association that the princes and free towns retained most of the rights of government over their lands, which limited the power of the monarch and made him more of a supreme judge and military commander than an active ruler of the German lands. No general measures could be introduced unless they had the consent of all, a notion that around 1500 was articulated as a fundamental constitutional principle governing the relations between the emperors and the imperial diet. This was an assembly of the princes and free cities which originated in the gatherings of nobles summoned to the royal court from time to time by the kings and emperors. Around 1500 its procedures were formalized, regular meetings were envisaged, and it was known as the Reichstag (literally, assembly of the estates of the empire). From 1663 the Reichstag remained in permanent session in Regensburg and the princes and cities sent envoys rather than attending in person.

The princes and free towns never became sovereign, however, and they remained subject to the higher authority of the emperor and imperial law until 1806. Indeed, from the middle of the 14th century, the empire developed institutional and legal structures which ultimately became more important than the feudal relationship between the emperor and his vassals. Throughout the empire's history its government was conducted by the monarch with the aid of a relatively small core team comprising the imperial arch-chancellor and other individuals, but the framework in which they functioned changed greatly. Gatherings of notables for royal elections gave way to the establishment of a college of seven designated electors. Gatherings of nobles at court became more formal 'court' diets (Hoftage) and then imperial diets (Reichstage) by about 1500. By the 16th century, too, justice by special session at gatherings of nobles presided over by the monarch himself was replaced by two supreme courts (the Reichskammergericht at Speyer and the Reichshofrat at Vienna), each staffed by legally qualified judges.

The link between the papacy and the empire loosened after the 14th century and was severely undermined by the Reformation. The papacy never in fact recognized the Peace of Westphalia of 1648, which finally confirmed the rights of Lutheran and reformed Protestants in the empire. The German imperial church (Reichskirche), a key instrument of imperial government under Charlemagne, was reduced to a core of mainly south-western and Rhineland supporters of the crown by the later 16th century. From 1519, finally, the powers of the monarch were formally circumscribed in a lengthy electoral capitulation which a newly elected emperor was obliged to sign before his coronation.

By the 18th century the accumulation of fundamental laws from the Golden Bull (1356) to the Peace of Westphalia (1648) was regarded as more than the equivalent of any other pre-modern constitutional regime. The rights that Germans held under these laws were more extensive and more explicitly coded in published legislation than those of the inhabitants of any other European polity. Furthermore, imperial law guaranteed that all German subjects had the right to appeal to a higher court, if necessary to the emperor himself, if their rights had been transgressed. They could thus take legal action even against their own rulers.

Territories

Charlemagne's empire straddled what are today France and the western part of Germany but it did not endure more than a few decades. The Saxon successors of the Carolingians shifted the kingdom further east while the western Franks laid the foundations for what soon became the French monarchy. The

Saxon kings were replaced by Franconian and Swabian dynasties, and by the 13th century the German kingdom was supplemented by the kingdoms of Burgundy and of Italy. The Luxemburg and Habsburg rulers once again shifted the focus, now to Bohemia and the Austrian lands in the south-east. By the 16th century, Burgundy had disappeared and all that remained of Italy was a small collection of north Italian fiefdoms—Habsburg Italy rather than Imperial Italy—that remained under imperial overlordship until 1806. The Swiss cantons effectively left the empire in 1505 and their independence of it, along with that of the Dutch Republic which had once been its Netherlands provinces, was confirmed in the Peace of Westphalia in 1648.

The lands of the German East which so preoccupied many nationalist German historians in the later 19th and first half of the 20th century were never part of the empire. The territories settled by the Teutonic Knights in the 13th century which became the duchy of Prussia in 1525 were a fiefdom of the Polish-Lithuanian Commonwealth and inherited as such by the electors of Brandenburg in 1618. They became sole rulers of the duchy of Prussia in two stages, 1657/60 and 1772, but it was never part of the Holy Roman Empire and only formally amalgamated with Brandenburg after 1806. The idea that the Germans had always been driven by a *Drang nach Osten* (a 'drive towards the East') was essentially an invention of the later 19th century when some German nationalists advocated the colonization of the East, allegedly following in the footsteps of their medieval forebears. The core of the early modern Holy Roman Empire from about 1500 was the old German kingdom.

Imperial coronations

The complexity of the empire's history from start to finish is exemplified by the absence of a centre and by the procedures for the election and coronation of its rulers. The empire never had a capital city. Its notional centre was simply the court of the individual who happened to be emperor at the time. From the mid-15th century that was by and large Vienna, though not continuously so until after the Habsburgs abandoned Prague as a place of residence and government after the death of Rudolf II in 1612. Vienna became the court centre both of the Habsburg lands and of the empire, and its significance was enhanced by the presence of the Reichshofrat, the emperor's supreme court, and the Reichskanzlei or imperial chancellery. As the seat of a major European dynasty its significance outshone all other German cities. Under the brief reign of the Bavarian Wittelsbach Emperor Charles VII (1742–5), neither Munich nor Frankfurt proved to be a plausible alternative to the Habsburg court.

Yet both the imperial diet and the other main court of law met elsewhere. For several centuries gatherings of nobles, the precursors of the late medieval Hoftag and the early modern Reichstag, were summoned to wherever the emperor happened to be. The Golden Bull of 1356 decreed that Nuremberg should be the location for the first diet of every reign, though this did not always happen. From 1663 the imperial diet resided in permanent session at Regensburg, which became an increasingly important diplomatic centre. The empire's other main court, the Reichskammergericht, paid for by the imperial estates, was established at Nuremberg but settled in Speyer in 1527, where it remained until a French invasion necessitated relocation to Wetzlar in 1689. Neither Speyer nor Wetzlar attracted anyone but judicial officials, lawyers involved in cases, and young aspirants such as Goethe in search of training in imperial law.

The empire had no natural ceremonial focal point. It is not known whether or how Charlemagne was either elected or crowned king of the Franks, but he was crowned emperor by the pope on Christmas Day 800 and he certainly insisted on the coronation of his son in Aachen in 813. The subsequent traditions of the empire remained deeply influenced by these two events. Medieval German rulers were first elected kings in Germany, then crowned emperor in Rome by the pope. There were no clear rules for the election of a king. The first Saxon king was elected in 911, following a deal between two (out of five) dukes, regional overlords in the Carolingian monarchy. His successors tended to be elected with the support of the dukes and other leading nobles. The precise number of those entitled to vote was unspecified until 1356 when the Golden Bull designated seven princes as electors; two more were added in the 17th century.

There was initially no fixed place of election, though Mainz and Frankfurt were most commonly chosen: the former because it was the seat of the imperial arch-chancellor the archbishop of Mainz, the latter because of its centrality and its ability to host, and pay for, large gatherings of notables and retainers. In 1356 the Golden Bull specified that Frankfurt would be the sole place of election, though some subsequent elections also took place at both Augsburg and Regensburg.

Until the 16th century, the coronation of the German king tended to take place in Aachen, followed by his imperial coronation at some later point in Rome. Initially the title conferred was *rex Teutonicorum* (king of the Germans) but this changed to *rex Romanorum* (king of the Romans) from the 12th century; the king then assumed the imperial title after his second coronation in Rome. Maximilian I was elected *rex Romanorum* in 1486 and he succeeded his father in 1493. His perpetual disputes with Rome, however, made a papal coronation impossible. From 1508 Maximilian thus simply assumed the title 'elected German emperor' ('Erwählter Römischer Kaiser'), as did all his successors until 1806. The only exception was his son, Charles V, who was the last emperor crowned by a pope. Since Charles's troops had virtually destroyed Rome in 1527, however, the coronation took place in Bologna in 1530.

From the later Middle Ages, the heir apparent was generally elected and crowned 'Roman king' before an emperor's death, though the election could take place simultaneously with the imperial election after an emperor's death, if necessary. With one exception, Charles VII who ruled for only three years from 1742, all Holy Roman emperors after Frederick III were Habsburgs.

After 1562 the imperial coronations took place in Frankfurt as well as the elections. One reason may have been the fact that, owing to an untimely death, there was simply no archbishop of Cologne to place the crown on the emperor. Frankfurt was also a large and prosperous free city with enough grand houses to accommodate those who needed to attend and it was closer to the Habsburg territories than Aachen.

The imperial insignia

To the end in 1806, the coronation involved the use of the same collection of insignia and holy relics that had been collected during the Middle Ages. Emperors were clothed in what was claimed to be Charlemagne's coronation mantle, though in fact the robe was probably made around 1133–4 in Sicily of silk imported from Byzantium, and it was first mentioned in German sources in 1246. A century later, however, it was already being referred to as Charlemagne's mantle and was complemented by other items, also largely of 12th-century Sicilian origin, such as the alb, the dalmatic or tunic, a stole, undergarments, belt, gloves, and shoes.

The same mythology had developed earlier about the imperial crown (see Figure 1), which was almost certainly made in the western Rhineland around 1024, and the orb, which was acquired by the Staufer emperors in the 12th century. Other items of the imperial insignia included the sceptre, sword, and the Holy Lance, which allegedly had embedded in its head a nail from the Cross, and which came into the possession of the German kings in the 10th century. Practically the only item with real Carolingian links was the so-called 'Coronation New Testament', an ornately bound, illuminated manuscript produced in the palace school at Aachen shortly before 800.

1. The Imperial Crown of the Holy Roman Empire, probably made in the lower Rhineland in the 10th or 11th century.

The imperial insignia and other items, together with various relics, such as a splinter of the True Cross and a fragment of the tablecloth used at the Last Supper, were initially handed down personally from king to king. They travelled frequently and were kept at various locations. In the 14th century Charles IV began the custom of displaying them annually. In 1423, when Prague was threatened by the Hussite uprising, Emperor Sigismund moved them from the nearby Karlštejn Castle to the Church of the Holy Spirit in the imperial city of Nuremberg, to which he gave the privilege of perpetual guardianship of the collection. The practice of annual exhibitions ceased when Nuremberg became Protestant in 1523, but the imperial insignia and relics remained there until they were removed to Vienna when French forces invaded in 1796. Hitler ordered their return to Nuremberg in 1938 but they were relocated to the Hofburg in Vienna in 1946, where they remain to this day.

The history of the imperial symbol of the double-headed eagle reveals a similar evolution. The single eagle of the Roman Empire also adorned Charlemagne's palace at Aachen. The Ottonians too used the single eagle, notably inscribed on a Roman cameo which was mounted amid jewels and pearls and items formerly owned by the later Carolingians on the cross which Otto III (r. 983–1002) presented to Aachen cathedral. Until the 14th century the single eagle sufficed to indicate the claim to Roman succession.

The double-headed eagle originated in Asia Minor in the 4th century and was increasingly used in the eastern or Byzantine Empire until the Palaeologus dynasty adopted it in the 13th century. It then began to be used in the Holy Roman Empire until Emperor Sigismund formally designated the black double-headed eagle on gold as the imperial standard in 1433. This was increasingly depicted with the arms of towns and princes on its feathers, initially organized in ten groups of four (hence its name, the *Quaternionenadler* or 'quaternion eagle') but later often including many more than ten groups. The double eagle could stand for the emperor (with the ruler's coats of arms on its chest) or for the empire (with a crucifix on its chest); it came to be widely used throughout the empire, for example in the coats of arms of imperial cities or in the pennants and documents of craft guilds.

Whether single headed or double headed, the eagle provided one of many enduring points of identification between German subjects and their rulers and the German polity. Many scholars in the 19th and 20th centuries denied that the empire ever generated patriotic enthusiasm or a sense of German identity among its inhabitants. A key theme of this book, by contrast, will be the identification of the empire with the German nation, which developed continuously throughout the Middle Ages. The definition of this German empire was further refined by the conflict over reform of the church which preceded the Reformation. This led many writers to deny the empire's Roman origins and to argue that it had really been a German empire from the outset. The empire's title remained unchanged and some Catholic theorists continued to believe in the idea of Roman origins and of a special relationship with the papacy but, increasingly, most dismissed this as myth.

The later Holy Roman Empire

By the 18th century the question of origins was less important than the consensus among both Protestant and Catholic commentators that the empire was a kind of federation. The German princes and cities exercised legislative power jointly with the emperor in the diet; the emperor, on the one hand still feudal overlord over the princes, acted on the other hand as a kind of supreme judicial official in overseeing that the laws thus jointly agreed were observed. This German polity was commonly referred to simply as 'the empire' ('das Reich') or 'the German empire' ('Deutsches Reich'), or even simply 'Germany' ('Deutschland').

This view of the empire was also widespread among major foreign commentators. Montesquieu visited the Holy Roman Empire in 1729 and concluded that it was a federation which worked effectively. Voltaire himself was more favourably inclined to the empire than is often assumed. His apparently disparaging characterization of the empire actually referred specifically to the conclusion of the reign of Charles IV (r. 1346) when he commented on the stabilizing function for the German kingdom of the Golden Bull of 1356, on the way that it limited the emperor's powers, and on Charles's apparent indifference to Italy and his acquiescence in the authority of the papacy. Voltaire understood the empire in his own day to be a republic of princes presided over by the emperor, a polity whose fundamental laws succeeded in limiting royal power and preserving German liberty. Its title was archaic and anachronistic in the 18th century; its system of government was not.

Observers in the 17th and 18th centuries found it difficult to classify the empire in relation to other European polities. Pufendorf famously opined that it was 'like a monster'. What he meant by that was simply that the empire could not straightforwardly be classified as a monarchy, an aristocracy, or a democracy, the categories of government that Aristotle had defined. 'Germany', as the great legal and constitutional commentator Johann Jacob Moser declared, 'is ruled in German'.

German historians in the 19th and early 20th centuries despised the empire for not being a nation state and blamed it for delaying the development of the Germans. They often praised the territories for their cultural achievements but refused to recognize the ways in which the empire made them possible. Critics of Germany before and after 1945 often sought to establish the continuity from First Reich to Third Reich, which cast sombre shadows over the centuries before 1806. More positive assessments of the empire since 1945, either as a transnational precursor of the European Union or as the first German nation state, have been criticized as strained and inappropriate.

At many points over the last two centuries, the narrative of the Holy Roman Empire has served the needs of the present rather than reflected the objective reality of the old empire or even the subjective experience of those who lived in it. This survey will present an alternative view. Organized as a chronological narrative, the book will show how the empire developed through very different phases over a thousand years.

Chapter 1

Roman Empire and German kingdom: from Charlemagne to the Ottonians

Roman and Frankish origins

When Pope Leo III crowned Charlemagne as *Imperator Romanorum*, emperor of the Romans, in Rome on Christmas Day 800, he was already the successful and powerful ruler of the Frankish kingdom, as well as king of upper Italy. To his title of *rex Francorum et Langobardum* he now added an imperial title that seemed to convey vast authority but was in fact vague. It was not clear then that his coronation in Rome presaged the emergence of a new imperial system. Yet it was an important turning point in the slow transition from the Roman Empire to what, several centuries later, would become referred to as the German empire or Reich.

The Frankish kingdom resulted from the decline of the Roman Empire and the establishment of the Germanic tribes of the Franks on its north-western periphery. The Roman Empire had reached its apogee under Trajan around AD 110. Soon, however, strains began to appear in the administration of this vast area, which stretched from western Europe to Asia Minor and contained perhaps as much as 20 per cent of the world's population.

Controlling this vast empire became increasingly difficult and it was progressively decentralized until Diocletian (r. 284–305) formally subdivided it, so that four emperors ruled simultaneously.

The competing ambitions of the four soon led to renewed instability before Constantine (r. 324–37), who became the senior western emperor in 310, established himself as sole ruler of both east and west by 324. He moved his capital to Byzantium and renamed it Constantinople, embraced Christianity, and established the principle of dynastic succession.

Yet the revival did not endure. Internal conflicts and attacks on the Rhine and the Danube by migrating northern warriors such as the Huns led to the empire being divided once again, this time into eastern and western parts, in 395. By then, Rome itself was under threat from the Goths, who sacked the city in 410, and the new western imperial capital was in Ravenna.

The eastern Byzantine Empire, with its capital at Constantinople, flourished for several centuries and survived until it was conquered by the Ottomans in 1453. The western empire, by contrast, suffered repeated invasions by various Germanic peoples. These were not Germans, as later German commentators often asserted: 'Germanic' was simply a generic term used by the Romans to denote the barbarian tribes which lived east of the Rhine and north of the Danube, an area they called *Germania*.

As Rome's authority declined, these tribes soon drifted west and south and even before the deposition of the last western emperor in 476, Germanic kingdoms had been established in Africa, Spain, France, Switzerland, Italy, and Dalmatia. The new Germanic kings continued to recognize the authority of the eastern emperor; they sought his approval for their kingdoms and none ever sought to usurp the imperial title; they also adopted his currency. But they ruled independently and their world was dominated by almost constant warfare and by the rise and fall of Roman, Germanic, and Hunnic warlords. Only gradually, between the 3rd and the 10th centuries, did various clusters of these tribes begin to develop a common ethnic identity and ultimately a common language. The two most important were the Franks and, later, the Germans.

The Franks originated as an amalgamation of several smaller Germanic tribes who migrated from the lower and middle Rhineland to northern Gaul in the 4th and 5th centuries. At first they worked for the Romans as soldiers, then with them as allies, marrying into the Gallo-Roman elite. When they supplanted the Romans as rulers, they retained the Romans' language, their roads, and their administration.

The Frankish tribes were unified by Clovis, the first ruler of the Merovingian dynasty (r. 481/2–511). An extraordinarily successful military commander, energetic and ambitious, Clovis published the *Lex Salica*, a law book, around 500, in which he referred to himself as the *primus rex Francorum*. The eastern emperor Anastasius I (r. 491–518) made him an honorary consul of the Roman Empire and recognized him as Frankish king in 508. One of the reasons why the emperor honoured Clovis was probably the fact that he had converted to Nicene Christianity or Roman Catholicism, the official religion of the Roman Empire since 380, while other Germanic leaders embraced Arianism or simply remained heathen. The link with Roman Catholicism certainly helped him win over the majority Roman population; he soon assumed the role of protector of the church and even convened a church council at Orleans in 511.

Although Clovis divided his realm among his four sons, the idea of a common kingdom endured. Each took a share of the core area, known as Austrasia (or the 'eastern lands') around Metz, and of Aquitaine. From their four capitals at Rheims, Orleans, Paris, and Soissons, some 200,000 Franks dominated the region between the Seine and the Somme. By about 650, Clovis and his successors had conquered much of Gaul with its six or seven million Gallo-Roman inhabitants and had even extended their dominion into Thuringia and Bavaria.

Merovingian rule rested on the foundations of friendship between extended family groups rather than on feudal structures. The overlapping bonds of loyalty, cemented by marriage agreements, formal contracts, oaths, and other public ceremonies, created a dense network of interdependent clans. These managed communal tasks, including defence, and generally resolved disputes by arbitration according to unwritten laws. Friendship was publicly performed in ritual procedures such as the great feasts which marked the end of a dispute.

The kings adopted the Roman system of regional administrators, appointing counts (*comes*) and, east of the Rhine, dukes (*duces*) to administer royal business. This system seems to have been sufficiently flexible to take account of local circumstances. The Alemanni of Swabia, for example, were allowed to retain their own system of law and the Bavarians, an amalgamation of numerous tribes who emerged in the region between the Danube and the Alps in the 6th century, also enjoyed considerable autonomy under their duke. The rulers' alliance with the church also enhanced their influence.

Four kings successively managed to reunite the various parts of the Frankish kingdom but thereafter repeated partitions took their toll. The frequent inheritance of minors required complex wardship arrangements and enhanced the authority of local elites. The latter ensured that, increasingly, counts were appointed exclusively from among the landowners of the relevant area, which accelerated their evolution from royal officials to quasi-autonomous local authorities. The greatest beneficiaries were the highest court officials, the major-domos, who increasingly acted as regents on behalf of the monarchy and forged extensive alliances within the Frankish nobility. By 751 the descendant of one such individual, Pepin the Short, became king (r. 751–68), having asked the pope for permission to depose the last Merovingian ruler, Childeric III (r. 743–51).

This shifted the centre of Frankish power away from Paris and the Seine region to the area between the Meuse and the Moselle, where Pepin held estates. He proved relentless in rooting out internal opposition and in attempting to regain control over Aquitaine, Swabia, and Thuringia. Wisely, he left the office of major-domo vacant.

Pepin's anointment by the papal legate Boniface gave his rule the aura of divine election and approval. Before long Pope Zachary (r. 741–52) asked for assistance against the Langobard or Lombard kings of northern Italy. Pepin's promise to secure the former Byzantine territories of middle Italy for the papacy led to a second anointment by Zachary personally in the Basilica of Saint Denis, after which he was styled *patricius Romanorum*, protector of the Romans and of the Roman Church. When he transferred the Exarchate (or province) of Ravenna into the hands of the pope he laid the foundations both of the future papal state and of a continuing cooperation between his dynasty and the papacy. Pepin's good faith was further underlined by his support for a mission to Frisia, for which he established a bishopric at Utrecht.

Charlemagne and the Carolingians

Pepin's endeavours bore fruit in the reign of his son Charles, later known as Charles the Great or Charlemagne (see Figure 2), whose achievements account for the fact that his dynasty is referred to as Carolingian rather than as Pepinid. In many ways Charlemagne (r. 768–814) simply carried out Pepin's programme. For over thirty years he fought the Saxons on his north-east frontier, finally subjugating them in 804. In Italy he pursued a successful campaign against the Langobardian kings, culminating in the wholesale slaughter of the Langobard royal family, the capture of the royal treasury and the elaboration of his title to *rex Francorum et Langobardorum*. By the end of his reign, in addition to Saxony and Lombardy, he had fully subjugated Aquitaine, Swabia, Bavaria, and Carinthia, and turned the Slav provinces to the east of his realm into dependent territories.

2. Charlemagne as imagined by Albrecht Dürer, 1514.

As in Pepin's reign, military offensives were complemented by careful attention to both secular and ecclesiastical administration. Charlemagne continued to appoint counts and now also appointed special governors in the various marches or frontier zones (*comes marcae* or margraves). Since these were invariably chosen from among the local nobility he also created a new type of royal official, the *missi dominici* or royal envoys: these had no permanent base but travelled on behalf of the monarch. The appointment of dukes, who had the potential to become strong regional leaders and challengers to the crown, now ceased.

At the same time Charlemagne promoted church reform and the establishment of monasteries, and paid careful attention to the appointment of bishops and other high ecclesiastical dignitaries. The church became a key agency of Carolingian government. Alongside Charlemagne's own residence at Aachen, episcopal centres such as Cologne, Mainz, Trier, and Salzburg were training centres for clergy who would also serve as administrators. Charlemagne's general concern to foster a moral and religious reform of his lands gradually attracted scholars and teachers to his court and to the key episcopal and monastic centres. Their main preoccupation became the copying of ancient texts, an activity facilitated by invention of a new script. The Carolingian minuscule was uniform and rounded, with capital letters and spaces between words, written on parchment rather than papyrus: it was relatively quick to write and easy to read. Over 90 per cent of all classical texts known to us today derive from these Carolingian scribes.

Yet these things contributed little to Charlemagne's acquisition of the imperial title. In 797 the eastern emperor, Constantine VI (r. 780–97), was deposed by his mother Empress Irene, leaving a vacuum in Constantinople not filled until Irene was herself overthrown by the Byzantine patricians in 802. In Rome in 799 Pope Leo III (r. 795–816) was attacked by his enemies who tried to render him incapable by blinding and maiming him. After being rescued by the king's envoys (*missi dominici*), Charlemagne escorted Leo back to Rome, where the pope publicly proclaimed his innocence of adultery and perjury and crowned the Frankish king as Emperor of Rome. Since Empress Irene could not be regarded as legitimate because of her sex, the proclamation was held to be justified.

The new eastern emperor, Nikephoros I (r. 802–11), refused to recognize Charlemagne for he himself still claimed the title Emperor of Rome. Yet Byzantium's disapproval made little difference. What mattered in the west was that Leo's action implied that he, the pope, held ultimate power. This question was to become central to the relationship between the emperors and the papacy until the 13th century.

That issue, however, only later became a bone of contention between rulers and papacy and it did not play a role during Charlemagne's reign. The Byzantine court might mock the self-important Frank with his barbaric and uncouth retinue, but Charlemagne's new title enhanced his prestige immeasurably. He already held two crowns (king of the Franks and the Langobards); the award now of the imperial crown set him apart from all other western rulers. The scope of his powers was not clearly defined; indeed he and his advisers only later settled on a precise title which expressed both ambition and ambiguity: 'Charles, the most illustrious Augustus, the great and peace-bringing emperor crowned by God, who rules the Roman Empire, and at the same time through God's mercy king of the Franks and the Langobards.' His immediate successors simply abbreviated this as *imperator augustus* or *rex* without an ethnic qualification (of the Franks, etc.), thus proclaiming their overarching authority over their various realms.

The next years marked the high point of the Frankish kingdom. Military success and the influx of booty taken from the vanquished had given the Frankish elites and their Gallo-Roman affiliates a sense of cohesion and identity. Tales of famous victories and of bravery and loyalty in battle generated myths of the prowess of Frankish warriors which united the disparate Germanic peoples and their cultures and legal traditions.

Yet the Germanic tribes still lived in a multilingual society in which Latin was the common language, supplemented predominantly by Vulgar Latin in the west and by Alemannic, Bavarian, and Saxon and other regional languages in the east. The imperial coronation endowed the monarchy with the aura of the Roman succession and an important sacral or religious dimension. Charlemagne viewed himself as the servant of

God whose wars were pursued in the service of a higher idea: the creation of the Kingdom of God on earth. The Franks consequently viewed themselves as God's chosen people, the representatives of good against evil.

Reality, however, soon undermined visions of a new world order. As an idea rather than a geographical reality, the *imperium* remained undivided under a single emperor. The *regna* or kingdoms, by contrast, were the terrestrial basis of the emperor's power and were subject to Frankish tradition which allowed both brothers and sons to lay claim to succession. Charlemagne's two eldest sons died in 810 and 811. The year before his own death in 814 and following the eastern Byzantine practice, he crowned his surviving son Louis co-emperor, without involving the pope but having gained the approval of the leading Frankish nobles. Louis the Pious (r. 814–40) achieved relative stability but his death led to a bloody civil war which ended in a tripartite division in the Treaty of Verdun (843). This created three kingdoms: western, middle, and eastern. The imperial title went to Lothair I, son of Louis the Pious, whose middle realm included the Italian kingdom.

This was the beginning of the end of the Frankish-Carolingian dynasty. The imperial title remained in the hands of whoever ruled the kingdom of Italy. By the end of the century, however, the Carolingians became extinct. For several generations the imperial title was passed around among several Roman families and ceased to have any real meaning. Between 924 and 962 there was no western emperor at all.

From eastern kingdom to German kingdom

Meanwhile, the eastern kingdom of the Franks, like the western kingdom which ultimately became France, developed a distinct sense of identity. Its rulers, the sons of Louis the German (r. 843–76), second son of Louis the Pious, successfully defended their claims against their uncles, thus establishing once and for all the succession rights of sons over brothers. They also took Lorraine, thereby pushing the western frontier back to a line formed by the Scheldt, the Meuse, and the Saône. The northern seas and Alps in the south formed stable natural frontiers, while in the east the frontier against the Slavs, from Carinthia, through the Bohemian Forest, up the Saale and the Elbe, remained constant.

The eastern realm was culturally backward compared with the western, but it was more successful militarily and it developed the elements of its own distinctive language. The Latin term used was *lingua theodisca*, though this did not mean 'German' in the modern sense. The word 'diutisc', first used in Latin translation in 786, simply meant 'common' and even when the term 'teutisci' appeared in 843 it simply denoted those who were not Langobards. The eastern Franks had no grammar or written language, but their sustained political union over several generations gradually created the basis for a common tongue distinct from the Romanic language of the western and southern Franks: a mix of Latin, Celtic, and various regional forms of northern and eastern Germanic.

After the Treaty of Ribemont (880) finally settled the boundaries between the eastern and the western Frankish kingdoms, Louis III (r. 876–82) established the capital of the eastern kingdom at Frankfurt am Main, whose central location helped him integrate the nobles of his lands into his court. And while his western Frankish counterparts lost control of the church to the papacy, Louis was able to retain the right to nominate bishops and control over church property.

Continuing internecine conflict, however, weakened the Carolingian dynasty and exacerbated a growing sense of crisis. On the eastern frontier the Great Moravian Empire posed a growing threat from the 830s, which persisted after Hungary overran that empire in the 890s; Viking raids penetrated the Rhineland around Aachen in 881 and down to the Moselle in

882 and 892. The last Carolingian king, Arnulf (r. 887–99), succeeded in becoming king of Italy in 894 and emperor in 896, but was unable to sustain the military initiatives required simultaneously in virtually every direction. His heir, Louis the Child (r. 900–11), was only six years old when he was crowned king at Forchheim in Upper Franconia in 900, and he was merely a pawn in the hands of the powerful nobles and bishops. The court itself was increasingly dominated by the bitter competition of the Conradines from the Wetterau and the Babenbergs from near Mainz for the dukedom of Franconia. Long after the award of the dukedom to Conrad, the Babenbergs remained eager for revenge.

As the monarchy faltered, the powerful eastern margraves, on whom the defence of the realm depended, gained in power. New leaders began to emerge from the ranks of the counts and other nobles and began to call themselves dukes. The Liudolfings of Saxony and the Bavarian Liutpoldings were particularly powerful malcontents. The new dukes became established in the traditional Germanic regions of Swabia, Bavaria, Thuringia, Saxony, Franconia, and, later, Lorraine, but they were not the direct successors of the Germanic dukes of the late Roman and Merovingian periods nor were they ethnic or tribal leaders. They were originally Carolingian nobles and they now asserted themselves to represent regional interests and to defend the integrity of the kingdom as a whole.

Their intense rivalry, however, nearly destroyed the kingdom they claimed to protect. With the support of Franconians, Saxons, Swabians, and Bavarians, the Conradines were able to secure the election of Duke Conrad as king at Forchheim in 911 (r. 911–18). He was the first non-Carolingian but, as a Frank, pursued the objectives of his Carolingian predecessors: to regain Lorraine from Charles the Simple, the ruler of western Francia, who had claimed it in 911; and to reassert the prerogatives of the monarchy against the powerful nobles. He failed in Lorraine. He partially achieved the second objective but he was handicapped by his lack of royal ancestors: without the aura of royal lineage, he was reliant on armed force; he died of a wound sustained in battle against Arnulf of Bavaria in 918. Since he had no male heir, the field was open for his enemies to arrange the election of Henry of Saxony as King Henry the Fowler (r. 919–36), so called because he was allegedly hunting birds when Franconian messengers arrived to inform him of his elevation.

The Saxon-German kingdom

Henry I's power base lay around Gandersheim, Hildesheim, and Quedlinburg, and his election represented a significant eastward shift of the centre of power of the eastern Frankish kingdom. He seems to have been chosen by a coalition of powerful Saxon and Franconian nobles who regarded him as *primus inter pares*; he himself declined anointment, which would have set him apart from those who had selected him. At first his power was limited, for the Bavarians elected their own anti-king, but his approach to such opposition was novel: after military threats he concluded a friendship treaty and within a few years had formally recognized all the dukes; unlike Louis III, he even acknowledged the dukes' authority over the bishoprics and monasteries in their lands. Equally novel was his decision in 929 to designate Otto, the eldest son of his second marriage, as his sole heir, thereby excluding three other sons from the succession.

The crown was no longer regarded as a family property to be divided among multiple heirs. The affirmation of the rights of dukes over their duchies would have made this impossible anyway. Yet when Henry arranged Otto's marriage to Edith, daughter of Edward the Elder of England, and then crowned and anointed him at Mainz in 930, he also signalled his determination to assert the singularity of the monarch above even the grandest nobles.

Otto I himself (r. 936–73) (see Figure 3) highlighted this theme in the ceremonies played out at Aachen when he inherited the crown

3. Otto the Great is regarded as the first German emperor.

in 936. Outside Charlemagne's chapel he was elevated by the leading nobles who swore their loyalty to him. In the chapel itself he was anointed and crowned by the archbishops of Mainz and Cologne. Then the dukes rendered service to the king symbolically at a festive meal by assuming the roles of steward, cupbearer, and so on. These offices were the basis for the ceremonial titles later held by the imperial electors.

For many years Otto was embroiled in bitter conflict with his brothers. His efforts to regain control over the church to restore its Carolingian role as agency of government and tool of royal patronage also generated tension, and his interest in Italy irritated Swabia and Bavaria which had aspired to take over the German role in northern Italy.

Italy and empire

Otto's Italian policy was piecemeal rather than the execution of a master plan to regain the kingdom of Italy and the imperial crown, but that was the ultimate outcome. The extinction of the Italian royal line in 950 left a vacuum which Margrave Berengar II of Ivrea attempted to fill by imprisoning the last king's widow, Adelaide, at Garda Castle and usurping the throne with his own son Adalbert as co-ruler. Berengar had become a vassal of the German king when he fled to Otto's court in 940 following a failed uprising against King Hugo of Italy. The prospect of him now establishing himself as the master of northern Italy clearly threatened the traditional claim of the German kings to the Italian crown and access to Rome. The situation was aggravated by the fact that Adelaide was the daughter of the king of Burgundy, in whose lands the German kings also had an interest.

Adelaide soon escaped and appealed to Otto for help. He swiftly inflicted a decisive defeat on Berengar, assumed the title of king of the Langobards, and, a widower since the death of Edith in 946, he married Adelaide in 951. The following year, however, he installed Berengar and Adalbert as kings under his overlordship and placed the marches of Verona and Aquileia under Bavarian stewardship.

An uprising led by Otto's own son Liudolf, who felt threatened by his father's new marriage, immediately jeopardized the new status quo. Liudolf was soon marginalized and deprived of his duchy of Swabia but the episode allowed the malcontents to make contact with the Hungarians, whose forces besieged Augsburg in 955. Otto's decisive victory over the Hungarians enhanced his prestige enormously and enabled him to respond to Pope John XII's call for help against Berengar's growing aggression. After securing the succession of his infant son by Adelaide by crowning him king, Otto marched south, took personal control of the Langobardian kingdom, and was crowned emperor in Rome on 2 February 962. Adelaide was crowned empress at the same time, the first medieval papal coronation of an empress.

Pope John XII (r. 955–64) himself had offered the coronation. It is no coincidence that a splendid copy of the forged Donation of Constantine was prepared at this time to show the new emperor: the document purportedly proved that Emperor Constantine had given authority over the western empire to Pope Sylvester I (r. 314–35) out of gratitude for having cured him from leprosy. Pope John saw the creation of a new emperor as an opportunity to enhance his own prestige and to reassert Rome's primacy.

Otto did not hesitate to accept. Even before he set off for Rome, his brother Bruno, archbishop of Cologne and imperial chancellor, designed a new imperial seal. The old image of the ruler as warrior with shield and lance was replaced by a frontal image which showed him bearing the insignia of crown, sceptre, and orb, the first medieval depiction of the orb which had been the Roman symbol of world domination.

Otto's ambitions were more modest. The relationship between the king and the papacy, between secular and ecclesiastical power, remained undefined: Otto recognized papal ownership of various Italian territories; the pope agreed that in future any pontiff elected by church and people should take an oath of loyalty to the emperor before his consecration. But many of the territories specified were not in fact controlled by either emperor or pope, and never had been. The idea of a papal oath of loyalty proved to be no more than a general reassurance that could easily be set aside.

Otto spent another ten years in Italy, where he consolidated his rule by creating new counts, reasserting royal feudal prerogatives, and building a new citadel at Ravenna, the old Byzantine centre. He failed, however, to persuade Basileus Nikephoros II Phokas (r. 936–69) in Constantinople either to recognize his title or to agree to a marriage between a Byzantine princess and his son. Nikephoros's successor, John I Tzimiskes (r. 969–76), was more amenable and Theophanu, possibly John's niece, aged about thirteen, married Otto II in Rome in 972. Marrying into the eastern imperial dynasty reaffirmed the primacy of the Saxon rulers over other western monarchs.

Imperial rule in Germany

North of the Alps, meanwhile, Otto set about consolidating his power by controlling episcopal appointments and endowing the bishoprics and other ecclesiastical foundations with land and rights. With papal permission he established a new archbishopric in 968 at Magdeburg with a suffragan bishop at Merseburg. The intensification of the Merovingian-Carolingian system of church patronage was now so pronounced that contemporaries referred to the German church as the Reichskirche, over which the king had authority as 'vicar of Christ'. Otto's generous endowments to the German bishoprics, monasteries, and convents stimulated what is often termed the 'Ottonian Renaissance', characterized by the foundation of cathedral schools and the production of new editions of the classical texts, as well as a wealth of new liturgical literature, the epic poems, sacred comedies and plays of the nun Hrothsvitha at the imperial convent of Gandersheim, and Widukind of Corvey's history of the Saxons and other works.

At the same time, the perennial struggle against the Slavs on the eastern borders gradually eased: in some regions Slavs entered into various forms of tributary contract with the German crown; Slav leaders such as the Bohemian Přemyslids and the Polish Piasts married into Saxon noble families and became margraves in the marches bordering their own lands; almost everywhere persistent Christian missions began to have a lasting impact.

Overall, Otto followed Frankish-Carolingian tradition. His monarchy was itinerant, reliant on the hospitality provided by the archbishops and other church leaders to enable him to travel around his realm. Indeed, such travel seems to have been more important to him than to his predecessors. Unlike the Carolingians he had relatively few officials; the old-style royal servants had now turned into hereditary aristocrats. The king's cultivation of a network of personal ties, friendships, and family relatives was crucial.

The written decrees and missives on which Charlemagne and his immediate successors had relied were now less important than rituals acted out in full view of the court. Grants of privileges and the like were made by means of ceremonies which enacted rank and status; the church services that marked Easter or Whitsun were events where power relations were played out by both king and nobles, the former asserting his authority, the latter accepting it. Otto I travelled largely in Saxony, to the Lower Rhine and to the central Rhine-Main region; his immediate successors extended the range to Swabia and other parts.

The eastern kingdom still had no formal title. Otto generally referred to himself as *rex*, later *imperator*, without specifying a specific territory or a subject people. His father's title had initially simply been king of the Franks and the Saxons, which excluded Swabia and Bavaria; Otto later styled himself, as Charlemagne had, *Rex Francorum et Langobardum (Italicorum)*, a ruler of people rather than lands.

Yet Otto's preference for a more general regal or imperial title did not break with tradition. After Charlemagne, the simple designation of the ruler as *rex* had become the norm in the eastern realm, while in the western realm the title of *rex Francorum* was used consistently from the 10th century. The difference perhaps reflected the greater uncertainty in the east about which parts the king actually ruled. Furthermore, the various chancelleries often used different styles, to which historians have often attached significance because they have suited their arguments concerning the emergence of a German monarchy or empire. In reality the Ottonians ruled over what essentially remained a Frankish kingdom into the 11th century.

New aspirations under Otto II and Otto III

Otto II (r. 973–83) also established his authority in an entirely traditional manner north of the Alps. At the start of his reign in 973 he was obliged to parry western claims to Lorraine and a northern challenge from Denmark. At the same time granting Swabia to his own cousin aroused the hostility of Bavaria, whose duke, Henry II (the Quarrelsome), he deposed in 976.

Yet there were signs of new aspirations. Having been crowned co-emperor in 967, Otto II's adoption of the title *Romanorum imperator* betrayed larger ambitions in Italy. In 980 he imposed his authority on Rome but his aim to take the south failed when he suffered a devastating defeat in July 982 at the hands of forces of the Muslim Emirate of Sicily at Capo Collone by Cotrone in Calabria. Nonetheless he was able to persuade the leading German and Italian nobles to elect his two-year-old son as king in Verona on Pentecost 983. This success was, however, overshadowed by a major uprising of the Slavs, which pushed imperial forces back to the Elbe; the emperor had no time to respond before he died in Rome in December 983.

The succession was secure, but only just. The deposed duke of Bavaria emerged to claim the guardianship of Otto II's infant son but was thwarted by the archbishop of Mainz and the Saxon nobility, who bought him off by promising to restore him in Bavaria. They insisted on installing the Empress Theophanu, who managed to stabilize the empire north of the Alps while renewing imperial claims in Italy and Rome. Following Theophanu's death in 991, Adelaide, the young ruler's grandmother, took over briefly until Otto III himself assumed power in 994, aged fourteen, and set about regaining lost ground. Having secured the loyalty of the Christian Obotrite Prince Mstivoj in Mecklenburg, he travelled to Rome where he installed his cousin Brun of Carinthia as Pope Gregory V and was crowned by him as emperor in 996.

A subsequent campaign against the Slavs east of the Elbe secured Otto's position north of the Alps sufficiently for him to place the government in the hands of his aunt Matilda, Abbess of Quedlinburg. He then returned to Italy where he aimed to break the power of the Crescentii clan in Rome and to make the city the centre of his power. He proclaimed a *Renovatio imperii Romanorum*, a renewal of the Roman Empire, and he adopted the title *Romanorum imperator augustus*. He also built himself a new palace on the Palatine Hill, where he introduced Byzantine court titles and ate alone on a raised half-moon table in the manner of the Byzantine emperors.

Even his decision to travel to Gniezno in 1000 to establish an archbishopric in memory of Archbishop Adalbert of Prague, who had died a martyr on his mission to the Prussians in 997, can be seen as part of his ambition to renew both church and empire.

As with his support for the establishment of the archbishopric of Esztergom in the same year, Otto aimed both to promote Christianity and, by securing recognition from the Polish and Hungarian rulers, extend his own *imperium*. When he returned to Rome, however, he was almost immediately driven out of the city by the citizenry. He died in January 1002 before he could retake it.

The succession of Otto III's second cousin, Henry of Bavaria (r. 1002–24), was challenged by several powerful noble aspirants, which no doubt reinforced his determination to proclaim a *Renovatio regni Francorum*. Though Henry also secured coronation as king of Italy in 1004 and the imperial crown in 1014—retaining the imperial title remained key—his priorities lay north of the Alps. Following Carolingian and Ottonian tradition, he founded a new bishopric in Bamberg and reinforced control over the church by promoting more royal chaplains to bishoprics than ever. He also struggled constantly against challenges to his authority in Lorraine and against the ambitions of Duke Boleslaw I of Poland in the east. His focus on Germany was reflected in contemporary references to him as the *rex Teutonicorum*, king of the Germans; he was the first ruler to be so styled.

With Henry's death in 1024, however, the Ottonian dynasty ended. Their achievement had been to construct a German kingdom on the foundations laid by their Carolingian predecessors and to maintain control of the church there. They had also secured the right of the elected German kings to the imperial title, though their control of the kingdom of Italy remained precarious and their authority over the papacy was limited. These issues were to play a central role in the rule of the Salian and Hohenstaufen dynasties over the next two and a half centuries.

Chapter 2

The high medieval empire: from the Salians to the Hohenstaufen

The early Salian kings

While the Ottonians established the link between the German crown and the imperial crown and claimed the Italian crown, the real focus of their attention was north of the Alps. By contrast, the Salian and Hohenstaufen dynasties who ruled until the mid-13th century were forced to look south as the issue of the relationship between empire and papacy became increasingly problematic.

Following Henry II's death in 1024, the bishops, abbots, and nobles summoned by his widow Empress Kunigunde to Kamba on the Middle Rhine swiftly chose a successor. Two cousins, each named Conrad, seemed eminently suitable. Both were descendants of Otto I and scions of a Franconian dynasty (known as Salians after the Franconian legal code, the *Lex Salica*) with a strong regional power base in the Middle Rhine region. The younger had more land but the elder's wife, Gisela, was a direct descendant of Charlemagne and a potential heiress to the Burgundian crown; he also already had a male heir.

Conrad II (r. 1024–39) soon faced opposition. He won over the Saxons by affirming their laws but the nobles of Lorraine resisted until the death of their duke in 1026. Conrad's stepson, Ernest II of Swabia, remained a perennial antagonist until his death in

1030, while the younger Conrad, the king's erstwhile rival, smouldered until he was awarded the duchy of Carinthia in 1035.

From the outset the new king was determined to establish his right to succession in Burgundy, which Henry II had held since 1006. When Conrad succeeded Rudolf III of Burgundy in 1032, the *imperium* rested on the threefold foundation of Burgundy, Germany, and Italy. Royal powers in Burgundy were limited but Conrad gained control over the main Alpine passes. At the same time he ruthlessly asserted his rights in Italy against regional opposition fomented by the north Italian princes. By 1027 he was recognized as king of Italy and progressed to Rome for his imperial coronation. The following year his son Henry III was crowned king of Germany at Aachen.

In Germany Conrad worked to contain the power of the dukes, partly by adopting a policy which also proved successful in Italy: supporting the efforts of the vassals of the secular and ecclesiastical princes to establish the heritability of their fiefs. He also exercised his authority more harshly than his predecessors. Previously, noble transgressors had only to apologize to be forgiven their crime; those who appeared before Conrad's court were almost invariably punished, a prospect that cowed many. Equally important, he sought to neutralize the threats posed by Bohemia, Hungary, Poland, and the Wendish territories in the north-east and to establish good relations with the major northern ruler, King Canute of England, Denmark, and (after 1030) Norway.

Conrad followed Ottonian ecclesiastical policy by asserting his right to appoint bishops and extract substantial fees from his appointees. Yet he rarely bothered to consult a synod, and if the nascent church reform movement flourished in the 1130s it was because of the patronage of Empress Gisela. She became regent when Conrad returned to Italy in 1037 to deal with a new crisis precipitated by the archbishop of Milan's high-handed treatment of his vassals and to resolve matters in southern Italy.

Conrad deposed the archbishop temporarily but failed to subjugate Milan itself. He was equally unsuccessful in the south. Byzantium continued to hold Apulia and Calabria; the Lombard duchies of Benevento, Capua, and Salerno existed free of imperial control; the Saracens ruled Sicily. The dominant actor was the Norman mercenary commander Rainulf Drengot, who had been hired originally by the Byzantine duke of Naples and created count of Aversa by him. Conrad acquiesced, thereby recognizing the first Norman foothold in Italy. Soon after returning north he died at Nijmegen in February 1039.

Consolidation and church reform

Like his predecessors, Henry III (r. 1039–56) began his reign with an extensive progress round the German and Burgundian kingdoms. By 1046 he had visited most parts of each realm at least once, despite being distracted by a seditious uprising of the dukes of Lorraine and renewed military assaults from Bohemia and Hungary.

Henry was even more ambitious than his father, and the increasingly interventionist nature of his government was reflected in the fact that the chancellery, the source of all imperial documents, ceased to be part of the imperial chapel and was now established as a political office under the management of the chancellor. Deeply pious and given to public demonstrations of penance for his sins, Henry saw himself as Vicar of Christ with a mission to pacify the world. The appeals he made between 1043 and 1046 for a perpetual peace resonated with a widespread peace movement in western Europe which had generated numerous local and regional pacts over the previous half century. But they also aroused suspicion, for Henry's harsh treatment of those who transgressed seemed to deny the rights of princes and nobles and even bishops.

Henry's early episcopal appointments showed that he favoured the cause of church reform. The movement originated at the

Benedictine foundation established at Cluny in 910 and gradually spread to the German monasteries, winning adherents throughout the church. The key issues were secular control over the church and the morality of the clergy: simony (selling or buying ecclesiastical benefices) and Nicolaism (clerical marriage), both formally prohibited by canon law.

Previous monarchs, like their vassals lower down the hierarchy, had practised simony as a matter of course: the fees paid by newly appointed bishops and other clerics were a vital source of income. By the 1040s attitudes had changed and Henry was among those who believed that this sin must be eradicated. His expedition to Italy in 1046, a logical sequel to his travel in Germany and Burgundy, provided the opportunity to act.

He aimed to receive homage as king of Italy in the north, secure his imperial coronation in Rome, and establish his authority in the south. He prepared the ground by making strategic appointments to the three major northern metropolitan sees of Milan, Aquileia, and Ravenna. On his arrival he summoned a synod of bishops to Pavia, where he denounced the sale of benefices. At another synod at Sutri in December he resolved a two-year-old crisis in the papacy by deposing three competing popes and installing Bishop Suidger of Bamberg as Clement II (r. 1046–7).

Following Henry's and his wife Agnes's coronation on Christmas Day, Clement excommunicated all simoniacs. The people of Rome gave Henry the title Patrician (*Patricius*), with authority over Rome and papal elections. He took this to mean that he had the right of nomination, which he subsequently exercised three times in favour of German bishops. In southern Italy he managed only to transfer the Norman warlords to his own direct vassalage, which failed to contain their growing power.

Henry received much posthumous praise for having restored imperial authority over the church and the three kingdoms.

Yet his intervention in Rome prompted many bishops to question his right to dictate to the church. Some argued that in the Donation of Constantine the Eastern Emperor had given overall authority over the west to the pope. Others denied that Henry's consecration was equal to that of a bishop and doubted the sacrality of his kingship.

These matters became burning issues in the long reign of his son who succeeded, aged six, as Henry IV (r. 1056–106). The regency of Empress Agnes was initially backed by the archbishops of Cologne and Mainz and the bishop of Augsburg. She also appeared to buttress her authority by awarding the three vacant duchies to potential opponents: Bavaria to the Saxon Count Otto of Nordheim; Swabia to Rudolf of Rheinfelden, who also married her daughter Mathilda; Carinthia to the Swabian Count Berthold of Zähringen, who had been promised it by Henry III. In fact the re-establishment of powerful duchies created hostages to fortune, but what really undermined Agnes's position was a serious blunder in her dealings with the church.

The cause of reform had made significant progress in Rome during previous decades. The campaign against simony and for celibacy had now become central to the papacy's sense of mission and both issues were combined in the rallying cry *libertas ecclesiae*, freedom of the church. Furthermore, Leo IX (r. 1049–54) transformed the role of the papacy. His predecessors had rarely left Rome; he travelled like a monarch and, in doing so, asserted the authority of the bishop of Rome over the church more stridently than ever before.

At the same time, the rise of the Normans offered potential military support both against local opposition in Rome and against the emperor. Nicholas II (r. 1058–61) attempted to reinforce the independence of the papacy by decreeing that the cardinals would henceforth elect the popes and that the acclamation of a pope by the Roman clergy and laity would be purely symbolic. The

Roman nobles and their supporters in the church responded by persuading Agnes to support the election of their own antipope. The reform-minded German bishops promptly sidelined her, however, and the archbishop of Cologne became de facto regent.

On coming of age in 1065, Henry IV faced serious problems in both Germany and Italy. Rumours of a conspiracy to assassinate the king led to Otto of Nordheim, duke of Bavaria, being summoned to an imperial court in 1070 and, after he refused to participate in a duel to prove his innocence, he was deprived of both his dukedom and his Saxon allodial properties (i.e. those which he owned outright, independently of any overlord). This harsh treatment precipitated a major Saxon uprising in 1073.

Otto profited from the opposition to Henry's regime in Saxony. Wherever possible, Henry had demanded the return of royal property previously given away. Like other lords at the time, he also extracted onerous payments from his fiefs and transformed former communal lands, such as woods, into lordship domains. The construction of hilltop castles exacerbated the sense of an oppressive concentration of power, for they seemed designed to dominate a region rather than, as before, to provide refuge for the population in emergencies. They were invariably manned by royal officials from Swabia and elsewhere, some of them, even, non-nobles; the king's insistence that they marry daughters of Saxon noblemen gave rise to complaints about the abduction and rape of Saxon women.

The Saxon duchy which had prided itself on being the main pillar of the Ottonian and early Salian monarchy now resented the king's frequent visits: many said that Saxony had been reduced to serving as little more than a kitchen, good only for the sustenance of the largely non-Saxon court.

Henry's refusal to hear the Saxons' complaints prompted an uprising. He fled west to Worms, where the townspeople had just driven out the bishop and welcomed his promise of privileges. His fortunes only really turned when a band of Saxon peasants desecrated the graves of members of the royal family, which split the Saxon opposition and persuaded south German princes and bishops to come to his aid. In June 1075 he crushed the Saxon and Thuringian peasants led by Otto of Nordheim and the rebel leaders were imprisoned and deprived of all their property. At Christmas a gathering of princes at Goslar agreed to elect his one-year-old son Conrad as king. Otto once more sought Henry's forgiveness and was restored to his duchy of Bavaria and made administrator of the duchy of Saxony.

Conflict with the papacy

Henry's victory proved hollow. Pope Gregory VII (r. 1073–85) had urged the Saxons to remain peaceful and loyal to their king, but he himself now turned against him. Building on the ideas of his predecessors, Gregory declared that Christ himself had founded the Roman church and that its bishop was St Peter's representative. He consequently claimed authority for himself and his legates over all other bishops, as well as the right to depose even the emperor and to release his subjects from all obligations to him.

Yet another crisis in Milan triggered action on these claims. A coalition of townsmen and lesser nobles (*valvassores*) demanded both church reform and participation in the government of Milan. In 1067 the rebels had undermined the episcopate of Guido da Velate, whom Henry III had installed in 1045, and secured papal support for their own candidate, Atto. Henry, however, appointed Gotofredo II da Castiglione, which had prompted Alexander II (r. 1061–73) to excommunicate all Henry's advisers. Still embroiled in the Saxon uprising, Henry apologized to Gregory and promised to eschew simony in future.

Following the death of the rebel leader Erlembaldo Cotta in 1075, Henry created his own Italian court chaplain Tebaldo da

Castiglione (r. 1075–80) archbishop and appointed new bishops in Fermo and Spoleto, both in the pope's own metropolitanate of Rome. When Gregory threatened excommunication, Henry summoned a synod to Worms, where twenty-four bishops renounced their obligations to Rome and supported a public letter demanding the pope's abdication. In the German version Henry referred to himself as the anointed of the lord; in the Italian version he styled himself Roman *Patricius*.

Gregory's response was draconian. He excommunicated Henry and deposed him, formally releasing his subjects from any obligation to him. Henry's weakness rapidly became apparent. A new Saxon uprising gathered ground. The murder of Duke Godfrey of Lower Lorraine in February 1076 had deprived him of a key ally. The Upper German dukes summoned a diet at Tribur in October 1076 to tame the errant king. Henry's episcopal support also evaporated, for few bishops were willing to defy the pope by following an excommunicate.

The presence of papal legates added spiritual authority to the diet's deliberations. The Saxon proposal to depose the king failed but it was agreed that he should be humiliated and subjected to the will of the princes. Encamped on the other side of the Rhine at Oppenheim, Henry was obliged to promise to obey the pope and to secure his release from excommunication within one year. Pope Gregory was to be invited to preside over a new diet at Augsburg on 2 February 1077 to consider the future of the kingdom.

Henry did not await that discussion. He set off over the wintry Alps to intercept the pope. On 27 January 1077 he appeared barefoot in his penitent's robe before the walls of Canossa Castle where Gregory had taken refuge with Countess Matilda of Tuscany. The same ritual was repeated on the two following days; Gregory then released Henry from his ban and gave him the kiss of peace before celebrating Mass with him.

German historians traditionally referred to the 'road to Canossa' as the greatest humiliation ever suffered by a German ruler. Their Italian counterparts presented it as the first great Italian victory, the first blow against German domination, which led to Italy's 'self-liberation' from the Holy Roman Empire in the 15th century. The truth is more prosaic. By travelling to Canossa, Henry effectively forced the pope to rehabilitate him though he had to recognize the pope's higher authority to judge him.

Neither Gregory nor Henry attended the diet which opened on 13 March. The princes resolved to declare Henry an unjust king and depose him; two days later they elected Rudolf of Rheinfelden, duke of Swabia. The princes thereby abandoned the principle of dynastic inheritance in favour of a free election (*electio spontanea*): in future no one would be elected simply because he was the son of the monarch. The discussions envisaged the kingdom as a collective entity comprising those who held responsibility for it: the princes had the right to decide who should be king. As hereditary monarchies began to emerge in France and England, the Germans thus took a decisive step away from the hereditary principle.

Most bishops, towns, and lesser nobles, however, distrusted the princes. The pope, too, while he recognized the princes' right to elect a king, disputed whether they could depose one. By 1080 Henry had re-established his authority in most of Germany except Saxony and demanded Rudolf's excommunication. Gregory responded by excommunicating and deposing Henry again.

Now, however, Gregory's enemies among the German and Italian bishops convened a synod at Brixen (Bressanone) to demand his abdication. They nominated Henry's former chancellor, Wibert of Ravenna (deposed and excommunicated by Gregory in 1078), as his successor. The Roman people opened their city gates as Henry arrived; Gregory was deposed and Wibert elected as Clement III (r. 1080–100). On Easter Sunday Henry and his wife Bertha were finally crowned emperor and empress. Meanwhile in Germany, Rudolf had died in October 1080 and his successor, Hermann von Salm (r. 1081–8), was unable to prevail outside Saxony and ultimately withdrew to his homeland in Lorraine.

Gregory attempted a comeback with the help of Norman forces but their plundering provoked a Roman uprising against him and he retreated to Salerno where he died in 1085. As Pope Gregory's star waned, the emperor's authority in Italy revived. In Germany, the death of Otto of Nordheim in 1083 left the Saxons leaderless. Carinthia and Swabia were awarded to loyal followers. The rebel Welf IV, duke of Bavaria, was deposed, but after he attempted an uprising against Henry in northern Italy in 1092 he was bought off with reinstatement as duke of Bavaria. When Henry promulgated a forty-year domestic peace in Germany with the support of the princes in 1103 he seemed to be back in control. Yet in 1104 his own son, Henry V, led a rebellion against him. Henry IV was obliged to abdicate; he escaped to Liège but died in August 1106 before he could launch a counter-offensive.

Henry IV had neglected to cultivate long-term relations with the upper nobility, relying on lesser nobles and royal servants or ministerials. His harsh treatment of offenders from the upper nobility gave him the reputation of being unjust and arbitrary in the exercise of his power. It was said that he was unreliable and morally corrupt; he was allegedly sexually perverse, unfaithful, and violent towards women. It is not clear whether this was true, but the fact that the accusations were made at all reflects his poor reputation and explains why he faced repeated rebellions.

Henry V (r. 1106–25) was initially warmly supported by the episcopate and the pro-reform princes, so there was hope that Rome might also welcome him. However, Gregory VII's successor, Paschal II (r. 1099–118), was now determined to abrogate all royal prerogatives over the church.

Henry's German allies fully supported the superiority of the kingdom over the church and the king's right to install bishops. In German tradition the bishops were, after all, the real pillars of the monarchy, agents of royal government, the monarch's most important supporters. Thus Henry sent the archbishops of Cologne and Trier to Rome in 1109 to argue the case for the German king's traditional rights. The pope countered that if Henry gave up his investiture rights the German bishops would return all the property they had received.

The bishops were incensed, and they stood by as Henry kidnapped the pope and the cardinals and forced them to confirm the king's investiture rights, promise that the pope would never excommunicate the king, and agree to his coronation as emperor. Victimizing the pope, however, soon once more turned the German bishops against Henry, and before long they were endorsing Paschal's demands.

Henry also faced other problems. Saxon nobles objected strongly to his energetic attempts to enforce his rule by building castles, employing ministerials, and seeking to enlarge the royal demesne by reclaiming fiefdoms which local families had expected to inherit. In the Middle Rhine region he clashed with Archbishop Adalbert of Mainz, in Thuringia with Count Louis and the duke of Saxony. All three were imprisoned for disobedience; the duke of Saxony was pardoned after a public act of capitulation; but the feeling that the king sought to humiliate his vassal rather than seek reconciliation rankled.

Things were better in Italy where Henry inherited the lands of Matilda of Tuscany in 1115. This further enlarged the fortune he had gained from his marriage to the twelve-year-old Matilda of England in 1114 (the engagement took place when she was just eight), whom he also managed to have crowned empress. News of a planned gathering of German princes, however, forced his hasty return to Germany. Having been excommunicated again, Henry was now forced to resolve the investiture issue.

At the 1121 Würzburg diet the princes insisted that he obey the pope. The following year the agreement later known as the Concordat of Worms distinguished between the ecclesiastical role of a bishop (the *spiritualia*) and the secular or temporal aspects (the *temporalia*). The king could endow a bishop appointed by a free election with his *temporalia*, i.e. make him a vassal. That, however, did not imply that the king was Christ's representative. Only the subsequent anointment and consecration by the relevant archbishop accompanied by two other bishops created a true bishop. Calixtus II (r. 1119–24) conceded only that the emperor might be present at elections of bishops and abbots in Germany and that following a tied vote he might tip the balance in favour of the person supported by the most senior electors.

Neither the monarchy nor the church really won the investiture controversy. Its most important outcomes concerned Germany. First, the bishops were no longer royal officials with unlimited obligations to the monarch; they became princes who owed feudal obligations to the king. Second, as the bishops' feudal overlord, the king gained new rights over the German church which compensated for the loss of reputation he had suffered. Third, the controversy strengthened the German princes. They failed to engineer a free royal election, but the principle had been established. They had prepared the compromise with the pope and then forced Henry to agree, bolstering their right to participate in decisions that affected the monarchy and the empire. The refusal of the duke of Saxony to sign underlined Saxony's continuing resistance to royal power.

The development of a German identity

In his correspondence with Henry IV, Gregory VII had referred pointedly to the *regnum Teutonicorum* or the *regnum Teutonicum*, which implicitly denied Henry any rights over Italy. The adoption of the term also reflects the development of German identity under Henry IV and Henry V. The internal conflicts of the period mobilized wider sections of the population than ever before: not only clergy, lesser nobles, and towns, but also peasants who supported the king against his internal opponents or against Rome. That could work against him too, as it did in Saxony, but the extent of popular support for the monarchy is striking nonetheless. The term 'diutisc' or 'diutsch' (the Old High German form of the modern word 'deutsch') was increasingly understood to mean subjects of the German kingdom rather than just the community of those who spoke the common tongue. The expression 'deutsche Lande' or German lands also came into usage in the late 11th century.

Germans continued to believe that the larger polity to which they belonged was the Roman Empire rather than a German empire and they developed myths of origins that explained how this had come about. The *Annolied* (Song of Anno), a posthumous eulogy to Archbishop Anno II of Cologne (d. 1075) composed around 1080, recounted that Caesar had been sent to fight the Germans and subjugated them after a ten-year struggle. In Rome he met with ingratitude and so he returned to Germany, where he was hailed as a hero. The Germans helped him conquer Rome and establish the empire, since which time Germans had been welcome there. The *Kaiserchronik* (Chronicle of the Emperors), probably composed about 1140–50, told a similar story and, reflecting the usage re-established by Henry V's chancellery, equated the *regnum Teutonicum* with the Roman Empire (*Romanum imperium*). According to this source, Charlemagne had first united the two kingdoms and the German kings had been emperors ever since.

The Staufer or Hohenstaufen

Italy also played a central role in the policies of the next major dynasty, the Staufer or Hohenstaufen. The electors initially chose

Lothar von Supplinburg, duke of Saxony (r. 1125–37). He was the clear favourite of the reformers but he was an old man of fifty. He failed to recuperate the Salian dynastic lands in Swabia or to defend papal claims against Byzantium, the Normans, and Venice. He was crowned in Rome in 1133 but his son-in-law, Duke Henry the Proud of Bavaria, was never recognized as his successor. Strongly supported by the papal legate, the princes opted for the modest but well-connected Conrad III of Hohenstaufen (r. 1138–52) rather than the boastful and more powerful Bavarian.

The Staufer of Swabia had established a power base in Upper Germany by remaining loyal to the crown when it was under attack from the dukes of Bavaria, Carinthia, and Swabia. Moreover, Conrad's mother, Agnes, was a daughter of Henry IV. Following his election as king in 1138 Conrad faced opposition from Henry the Proud and Welf VI of Bavaria, which was only slowly mitigated by calculated marriage agreements, though his dispute with Welf remained unresolved. Overall his reign was perceived as a period of war and uncertainty, marred by the total failure of the Second Crusade and another crusade against the Wends in the southern Baltic coastal regions in 1147–8. It was also blighted by a great famine in 1151.

Yet Conrad laid the foundations for future developments. The royal chancellery continued to develop as the key instrument of government, now under the active management of a non-clerical royal appointee rather than the arch-chancellor, the archbishop of Mainz; such was the prestige of the office of chancellor that its incumbents were often rewarded with archbishoprics when they left office.

Royal revenues were enhanced by recovering former royal properties and by acquiring new ones. Some became important residences, and the king's travels now invariably featured the great fortresses that were constructed at Hagenau, Gelnhausen, Nuremberg, Eger, Frankfurt, and Wimpfen, in addition to the old residences, such as Aachen, Goslar, and Kaiserswerth. His growing reliance on royal officials or ministerials and lesser nobles also slowly created a network of crown vassals that ultimately replaced the old system of duchies. Although Conrad was the first German king since 962 who was not crowned as emperor, his chancellery habitually referred to him as *imperator Romanorum*.

Frederick I Barbarossa

Conrad's successor, his nephew Frederick I Barbarossa (r. 1152–90), followed his uncle's example. He immediately proclaimed a perpetual peace in Germany, the first of several during his reign. He created new dukes, margraves, and landgraves, which further undermined the position of the traditional German duchies. By the 1170s the court regarded all the ecclesiastical and secular vassals as princes of the empire; Barbarossa himself compared them with the Roman College of Cardinals: supporters and advisers of the crown.

Traditional accounts of Barbarossa's reign emphasized his supposed long-running feud with his cousin Henry the Lion, duke of Saxony and Bavaria. Henry was much wealthier than the king and often behaved regally. But their relationship was good until 1179 when the Saxon bishops and nobles denounced the duke as a tyrant. This prompted Henry's arraignment before an imperial court, and when he refused to answer the charges against him he was outlawed and deprived of all his property. While Henry's substantial allodial properties (the properties he owned independently of any higher authority such as the king or emperor) were returned to him after his submission in 1181, his vassals were all transferred to the crown, which extended royal authority across the whole of northern and eastern Germany.

Developments in Burgundy also buttressed Barbarossa's position. Royal power there was mostly exercised by the powerful Zähringen dynasty from Swabia. Following Barbarossa's marriage to Beatrice, the heiress to prosperous Upper Burgundy, as his second wife in 1156, however, he dispensed with the services of his deputy. Though he removed Upper Burgundy from the kingdom again in 1169, turning it into the imperial fiefdom of Franche-Comté, his interest in Burgundy endured and he was crowned king at Arles in 1178. Burgundy still had some strategic significance for imperial control over the Alpine passes, but perhaps the most important benefit of his marriage to Beatrice was the money that enabled him both to compete with the duke of Saxony and Bavaria and to pursue the Italian campaigns that became so central to his reign.

German historians in the 19th century often reproached the Hohenstaufen for pursuing glory in Italy at the expense of Germany. Such arguments, however, reflected the national preoccupations of modern times. The medieval empire was understood as the totality of its three constituent kingdoms. An *imperium Romanorum* without Rome was unthinkable. Frederick achieved his imperial coronation in 1155, more swiftly than any previous king, and he made no less than six expeditions to Italy, spending over a third of his reign there to re-establish the *honor imperii*, the rights of the crown. The obstacles to his success lay in renewed conflict with the papacy over jurisdiction, the problems of the kingdom of Italy, and the advance of Norman power in the south.

In the Treaty of Constance 1153 the emperor promised to defend the possessions of the papacy and not to make peace with either the Romans or the Normans without papal approval. The pope undertook to support the crown and to sanction those who harmed it. Both parties agreed to make no concessions in Italy to the Byzantine emperor. They soon disagreed, however, over the question of the formal relationship between pope and emperor.

In a letter of protest at Barbarossa's abduction and imprisonment of the archbishop of Lund in Burgundy in October 1157, Hadrian IV (r. 1154–9) reminded the emperor he had endowed Barbarossa with his powers. But his reference to the empire as a *beneficium*, perhaps maliciously translated as 'fiefdom' by the imperial chancellor Rainald von Dassel, aroused consternation at court. Barbarossa vehemently rejected the pope's claims; his advisers argued that the pope's only function was to crown the person whom the German princes elected as emperor.

Barbarossa's attempt to force the issue led to nearly two decades of strife. Along the way, Alexander III (r. 1159–81) twice excommunicated him and ultimately obliged him to engage in a three-week process of public apology and obeisance in Venice. Canossa had been a pleasant stroll in the winter sunshine compared to this.

Managing the kingdom of Italy also proved difficult. By supporting some smaller towns against the tyrannical behaviour of Milan, Frederick simply incurred the animosity of others. Throughout middle and northern Italy the towns had developed a strong sense of communal identity in the later 11th century; their fierce pride in their autonomy could just as soon turn against the emperor as against the local hegemon in Milan. Furthermore the nobles had developed a similar autonomy and often made common cause with the towns against any royal intervention.

In 1158, at a diet at Roncaglia by the banks of the Po near Piacenza, Barbarossa commissioned a review of the crown's rights in Italy. Seeking to remedy the diminution of royal prerogatives under absentee monarchs since Henry IV, his commissioners used Roman law precepts to assert the uniform higher authority of the monarch over the kingdom, including traditional regalian rights over coinage, tolls, and taxes as well as overlordship over all fiefs, even if they had been sold. The Roncaglia programme was intended to re-establish royal authority in all three kingdoms, but even applying it to Italy was problematic.

Milan was only temporarily subjugated at the end of Barbarossa's second expedition (1158–62). By 1164 he was confronted by the

League of Verona comprising Verona, Padua, Vicenza, and Venice, and from 1167 he faced the hostile Lombard League with some twenty-five members, including Milan. It was not until 1183 that Barbarossa made peace and turned the Lombard League into an instrument of imperial policy.

Meanwhile, efforts to recuperate royal rights had generated friction with the papacy, since Frederick now claimed authority over towns in the papal lands, and even over Rome itself. The dispute was resolved in 1189 but the emperor still refused to recognize a distinct papal territory exempt from his authority.

Relations with Rome were further complicated by the growing power of the Normans south of Rome. In 1130 the papacy had assisted the creation of the Norman kingdom of Sicily and it played Sicily off against the emperor when the need arose. Threatened by a Byzantine army in 1150 and expelled from Rome by the local population, Hadrian IV concluded the Treaty of Benevento with William I of Sicily in 1156. This recognized William's kingship over Sicily as well as his possession of all peninsular Italy south of Spoleto and the papal lands.

With Sicilian support, Hadrian's successor, Alexander III, survived the challenge of four antipopes. Norman rule in Sicily was stabilized under William II (r. 1166–89) and the Byzantine threat receded. Barbarossa's only remaining option was an alliance with Sicily in 1186 when William's aunt, Constance, married Barbarossa's son Henry VI (r. 1191–7), with the provision that Constance be designated the childless William's heir. This was worth little at the time, for William was only thirty and his wife twenty, but it laid the foundations for the last and most spectacular attempt to establish a truly Roman Hohenstaufen empire only a few years later.

Barbarossa was celebrated in the 19th century as the founder of the German empire, but he was nothing of the kind. He aimed to establish a Roman empire that could compete with the church. Significantly, the term *sacrum imperium* was first used by his chancellery in 1157 to denote an empire that was sacred in itself, independently of the papacy; around 1180 the title *sacrum Romanum imperium* was used. Barbarossa fostered the cult of Charlemagne and had his antipope, Paschal III (r. 1164–8), canonize his great predecessor in 1165. The cult persisted long after the Third Lateran Council abrogated the canonization in 1179.

Barbarossa's veneration of Charlemagne as the great enemy of all unbelievers emphasized Charlemagne's supposed plans for a crusade. In that at least Barbarossa came close to his role model. When the Third Crusade was announced following the fall of Jerusalem in 1187, Barbarossa took the cross at Mainz and set out with 20,000 knights and 80,000 men. He never reached the Holy Land, for he drowned while crossing the River Saleph in southern Turkey on 10 June 1190. The fact that his bones subsequently disappeared soon gave rise to the myth that he had not died at all.

He had at least ensured the coronation of his son, Henry VI, as German king in 1169 so that Henry could be consecrated and crowned as emperor on Easter Sunday 1191. The key to his reign was that his wife was a claimant to the throne of Sicily. Following William II's death in 1189 it was usurped by Constance's nephew Tancred of Lecce (the illegitimate son of Duke Roger III of Apulia), but Tancred's death in 1194 finally left Sicily in the hands of the Hohenstaufen and Henry had himself crowned king in Palermo.

Frederick II and failure in Italy

Knowing that his son Frederick would succeed him in Sicily, but not necessarily in Germany, Henry VI (r. 1191–7) proposed transforming Germany into a hereditary monarchy and appeared to indicate that he intended to make Sicily the fourth kingdom of the empire. His ultimate aim was grander still: to be the 'peace emperor' who would reconcile east and west, conquer the heathens in the Orient, convert the Jews, and usher in the end of the world. The German princes were promised that their fiefdoms would become hereditary; the pope was offered the most lucrative benefice in every German bishopric. The princes, however, baulked at these plans, though they subsequently elected the infant Frederick as their king without demur. Henry, meanwhile, had mustered forces for a new crusade but succumbed to malaria at Messina in September 1197 before they departed.

Henry VI's early death destabilized Hohenstaufen rule in both Italy and Germany. The young Frederick was crowned king of Sicily at Whitsun 1198 but his mother's death later that year left the regency in the hands of Pope Innocent III, who swiftly removed the papal lands from imperial control. In Sicily, regional warlords schemed to enlarge their landholdings and competed for influence over the young ruler, weakening central power. In Germany, an anti-Staufer movement gained ground, resulting in the double election of Philip of Swabia, Barbarossa's younger son, and Otto IV, son of Henry the Lion, resolved by Innocent in favour of Otto, who was crowned at Aachen in July 1198.

The pope's intervention was accompanied by claims regarding the rights of the papacy in imperial elections. This incensed the German princes who regarded themselves as the rightful electors of the German kings. Decisively, Otto was supported by the three Rhineland archbishops and the count Palatine. This core group had often voted first in previous elections; now they took the initiative in a disputed election, a crucial step towards the formation of a specifically defined group of imperial electors. Yet Otto's energetic approach soon provoked opposition in both Germany and Italy, and by 1212 he was deposed in favour of Frederick of Sicily, the 'child of Puglia', as the *Kaiserchronik* called him, whose government was effective from his coronation as king in Aachen in 1215.

remictimus gratiose et relaxamus ac ettā
liberamus dictum Andream de claramon
te et omnes suos consanguineos familiares
seruitores & sequaces ab omnibus offen
sis iniuriis et excessibus per eos et eorum

4. Frederick II's efforts to secure Italy ended in failure.

Frederick II (see Figure 4) spent almost his entire reign in Italy.
He left Germany in 1220 and returned only in 1235–6 and 1237.
He transformed the government of the Sicilian kingdom with
the groundbreaking constitution of Melfi in 1231, the first
comprehensive code of administrative law since Justinian's in
the 6th century. Like Henry VI, Frederick II developed a grand
vision of the world-historical significance of his rule, and he
defied the pope and incurred excommunication by uniting Sicily
with the empire.

Was Italy more important to him than Germany? Germany was
crucial, for possession of its crown was the precondition for
Frederick's imperial coronation in Rome in 1220. The succession
was equally important. By the time he left for Italy he had ensured
that his son Henry VII (b. 1211) had been elected king and was
installed as duke of Swabia and rector of Burgundy. When Henry
later showed signs of independent ambition in Germany and

allied himself with his father's Italian enemies in the early 1230s, Frederick replaced him with his younger son Conrad.

Yet Frederick did not simply use Germany to promote his Italian ambitions. In his early years of itinerant kingship in Germany he followed the traditional policies of German kings. He extended his royal progress beyond the Upper and Middle Rhine regions to include Ulm, Augsburg, and Nuremberg. The areas of direct royal property ownership now included Alsace in the west and the Egerland and the Pleissenland adjoining Thuringia and Bohemia in the east. Royal government was largely carried out by officials and ministerials under the supervision after 1220 of regents, first the archbishop of Cologne and then the duke of Bavaria. In 1225 the Golden Bull of Rimini underlined the crown's continuing support for eastern colonization and Christianization by granting privileges and protection to the Teutonic Knights, though there was no question of these eastern lands being incorporated into the empire or formally 'colonized' by it.

Frederick avoided confrontation with the nobility. In his first years he established thirty-nine towns in south-west Germany alone, which indicates both the vitality of urbanization in Germany at this time and the continuing pressure of royal recuperation policies. In 1235, he issued a new imperial peace at Mainz: unlimited in time, reiterating royal prerogatives while at the same time confirming the rights of the princes. Until his position in Italy began to crumble in the 1240s, Frederick made the German system work effectively.

Italy was an entirely different matter. First, he had to secure Sicily. Then he became embroiled in conflict with Milan and the Lombard League. Problems with the papacy were postponed by the pope's wish that Frederick would lead a crusade, for the Fourth and Fifth Crusades (1201–4 and 1217–18), in which no monarch participated, had failed. Frederick promised a crusade in 1225 but its postponement led Honorius III (r. 1216–27) to excommunicate him, though he conquered Jerusalem nonetheless and crowned himself king there in 1229.

The papal ban was lifted in 1230 but in 1239 Gregory IX (r. 1227–41) imposed another one after Frederick invaded Lombardy; in 1245 Innocent IV (r. 1243–54) also deposed Frederick for good measure. Both emperor and pope pursued the controversy as a holy war: the emperor fighting as 'hammer of the world' (*malleus mundi*) to return the church to its original condition; the pope waging war against the antichrist, the 'brood of vipers' on his threshold. With Frederick's death in December 1250, however, the conflict ended. His heirs failed to survive in either Italy or Germany. The Hohenstaufen imperial vision, born of the inherited aspirations of the Ottonians and Salians, had failed.

Chapter 3
The later medieval empire: the emergence of the Habsburgs

The electors

Older histories of Germany generally referred to the period after the end of the Hohenstaufen as the 'end of the age of emperors', allegedly the start of what was portrayed as the long decline of the Holy Roman Empire. The end was, in fact, over five centuries away. But it is true that between 1250 and 1312 no German king was crowned emperor and that until 1493 only one was succeeded by his son. From 962 to 1250, the empire had been ruled sequentially by three dynasties; now, following two decades of weak kings, the so-called Interregnum, several dynasties competed for the German crown before the Habsburgs emerged as dominant in the 15th century.

It was precisely in this period, however, that the German kingdom evolved constitutional structures which institutionalized the elective monarchy. The most important was the establishment of a formal group of royal electors. Previously, participation in royal elections had been variable: first, election by the people divided into tribal groups, then by gatherings of ecclesiastical and lay princes. By the late 12th century it was accepted that no election could be valid unless the three Rhineland archbishops of Cologne, Mainz, and Trier and the count Palatine of the Rhine had participated, with the archbishop of Mainz playing the key coordinating role. Eike von Repgow's *Sachsenspiegel* ('Saxon Mirror') law compilation of *c.*1220–35 noted that the duke of Saxony and the margrave of Brandenburg were also among the privileged electors.

These six had the right to vote first; after them, any other bishops or princes present could also vote. The entitlement of the six, Eike explained, derived from the largely honorific royal court offices they held since the coronation of Otto I in 936: the arch-chancellors of Germany (Mainz), Italy (Cologne), and Burgundy (Trier), and the steward (count Palatine), marshal (Saxony), and treasurer (Brandenburg).

Before 1250 elections had usually followed the dynastic principle: a new king had to be a blood relation of his predecessor and he was almost invariably the person designated as heir by the previous monarch. With the extinction of the Hohenstaufen, free election was inevitable and that ultimately required a more formal electoral system and majority votes. This may have been the reason why the king of Bohemia (cupbearer), excluded by the *Sachsenspiegel* because he was not of German birth, now became the seventh elector. In 1257 the seven acted alone for the first time, but the rules were only formalized in the Golden Bull in 1356. Elections occurred in Frankfurt, coronations in Aachen; majority votes were recognized, provided at least four electors had been present; the electorates could not be subdivided nor could the number of votes be multiplied by a dynasty claiming the equal entitlement of two members of equal status.

In 1338 the electors declared at Rhens on the Rhine that the person they elected was entitled to call himself king of the Romans and to rule in Germany without further reference to the pope. A century later they were meeting as a separate college in the imperial diet, another reflection of their growing sense of themselves as pillars and guardians of the empire. At the same time the emergence of the diet as a more formal body also reflected the development of a more elaborate constitutional framework.

The new challenges of monarchy

The post-Hohenstaufen era posed new challenges for potential monarchs. The king needed to be both a military commander and a peacemaker. He had to secure the loyalty of large numbers of retainers, advisers, and supporters, enticing them with rewards but also on occasion disciplining them with ruthless brutality. Both he and his itinerant court had to project power and mastery; he had to be an imposing sovereign figure, a supreme judge with authority.

New royal castles were now much grander and more imposing. The new court etiquette that spread to Germany from France in the 1170s and 1180s also dictated more elaborate clothing, skill in behaving at court festivals, or engaging in jousts and the other games of the medieval knights; the rituals of courtship were as complex as the rituals of combat. Pressure on the monarch was increased by the need to compete with the larger territorial courts in the empire. The more powerful nobles also invested in imposing buildings, lavish courtly rituals, and sponsorship of troubadours and other court entertainers.

Kingship had never been cheap but the costs now soared. Without regular taxes, finance was a permanent headache. Traditional sources of income remained essential: the money and goods in kind that flowed from the royal treasury or from the bishoprics and abbeys which were essential staging posts in the kings' itineraries or which provided sustenance for royal sojourns nearby. The church also rendered other *servitia* (services), including men and money for military campaigns. The most lucrative payments in the 12th century had been those from Lombardy because they were invariably paid in cash, which seems to have been a growing trend in Germany in the 13th century as well. The consolidation or recuperation of royal property was always in tension with the necessity to raise money by mortgaging or pledging it.

The crown also competed with the nobility in establishing mints and founding towns, with charters guaranteeing their freedom and subordination only to the emperor himself. The Hohenstaufen had established Jewish communities in their imperial towns and in 1236 Frederick II declared that all Jews in Germany were under royal protection, which meant of course that the crown could turn to them for levies, loans, and help with currency management. From around 1300 authority over the Jews was devolved to the princes, though by then the largest and wealthiest communities were those in the free or imperial cities. In 1415 Emperor Sigismund tried to regain the protectorate over the Jews and impose a tenth penny tax on them, which might have amounted to one-third of their income.

These developments reflected key characteristics of the evolution of the German monarchy in this period. The English and French monarchies sought to accumulate as much land and power as possible, governing through the creation of central bodies staffed initially by clerics. The German crown appointed unfree ministerials or crown agents to whom the functions of government were delegated. The Concordat of Worms had turned the bishops into vassals and in 1231 Frederick II had confirmed the rights of all princes, both secular and ecclesiastical. The old tribal duchies were gradually fragmented and transformed into fiefdoms. This marked the beginning of an extraordinary proliferation of the feudal system in Germany. While some counts managed to join the upper nobility, most former ministerials and the free townspeople came to be integrated into a multi-tiered system of vassalage.

In political terms, and in the absence of a written constitution, the order of ranks was a way of visualizing and acting out the complex hierarchy of the empire. The earliest written description of the system in the *Sachsenspiegel* elaborated a *Heerschildordnung* (literally, a 'ranking of military shields'), with seven ranks from the king down to ordinary free men. Regional variations meant that this scheme was never more than an idealized version of reality. Nor was it a static structure: the monarchy itself adjusted the hierarchy, for example by creating princes and, in the later Middle Ages, new dukedoms. Yet the *Heerschildordnung* nonetheless articulated the empire's structure and the nature of the ties that bound the nobility to the monarch.

Feudalism and the territories and cities

The main practical consequence of the development of the German feudal system was the devolution of government to the territories and imperial cities. Broadly speaking, the seven electorates, seventy ecclesiastical and twenty-five secular principalities, roughly eighty free or imperial cities, and other small entities all developed governmental functions more or less in parallel; only the very smallest territories of the imperial knights lagged behind. Most of the others assumed key governmental rights that elsewhere in Europe belonged to the crown: the administration of justice, tolls, a mint, the guarantee of safe conduct (and the right to charge for it), and so on.

This did not endow the territories with sovereignty, for the term *Landeshoheit* meant government subject to the empire and the authority of the monarch. In some parts, larger and more concentrated principalities developed written legal codes from the early 14th century. Many other principalities became rather fragmented: agglomerations of lordships and jurisdictions, some owned outright and others held as fiefs, constantly changing as a result of marriages, partitions, purchases, sales, or mortgage and lease agreements. Many, if not most, owned jurisdictional rights that lay on land owned by someone else, just as some of their own lands frequently fell under another's jurisdictional right. In much of the south-west of the empire this pattern prevailed into the early modern period.

The apparent drift in the empire towards fragmentation was balanced by developments which aimed to preserve peace. The imperial *Landfrieden* or peace ordinances of 1103, 1152, and 1235 expressed aspirations but were not effective, or only intermittently so; nor did they say much about how or by whom breaches of the peace would be punished. Nonetheless the general peace legislation was renewed by Rudolf I (r. 1273–91) and from the early 14th century such initiatives proliferated on a regional basis throughout the empire and some larger territories began to issue their own *Landfrieden*.

Other forms of peacekeeping organizations also developed. As early as 1226 a Rhenish league of royal and territorial towns formed, followed by a Wetterau league of four royal towns in 1232. A second and larger Rhenish league formed in 1254. In the north, the Hanseatic League, which originated in associations of merchants from about 1160, developed into a league of towns by the mid-14th century. It was dedicated to the protection of trade routes from the eastern Baltic to the North Sea and it proved more durable than most others, surviving into the early 17th century. From the 14th century, leagues formed by princes, counts, and knights also flourished.

The Perpetual League of Schwyz, Uri, and Unterwalden formed in 1291 renewed an earlier association and aimed to secure the best route to Italy over the St Gotthard pass against feuding lords in the valleys. It developed into an extensive self-defence association against the incursions of Habsburg overlordship, with military forces and, from 1315, a diet (*Tagsatzung*) which met as required. It was the core of the Old Swiss Confederacy that formally left the empire in 1505.

A plethora of local and regional arrangements also existed. Noble dynasties formed marriage, inheritance, and mutual defence agreements. These created a web of relationships which acted as a deterrence and as sources of support in a crisis.

Interlocking territories and overlapping jurisdictions and the ceaseless to and fro of land and other transactions created the need for local agreements on conflict resolution and provision for arbitration tribunals.

None of this prevented disputes, of course, and some inevitably ended in violence. Yet the empire was more stable and more cohesive than has often been claimed. The sense of a common identity among its noble, ecclesiastical, and urban elites—perhaps up to 10 per cent of a population of 14–15 million in 1340—was further reinforced by the crisis of the monarchy but also by the experience of being part of a distinctively German polity. During the 13th and early 14th centuries, the German language began to be used more frequently in legislation and in the correspondence issued by the imperial chancellery. Language acted as a unifying and identity-creating factor and references to the 'German lands' became routine.

Regional and local loyalties remained strong but myths of common origins and of a common past also proliferated. While France developed a cult of the monarch and the royal bloodline, German identity developed around the belief that God had chosen the German people to be the heirs to the Romans. Their elected king automatically became emperor and it is striking that imperial affairs figure prominently in 13th- and 14th-century writings throughout the empire. Indeed, in vernacular writing it was common to use the same word, *riche* or *Reich*, for both German kingdom and Roman Empire. At the same time the clashes of the monarchy with the papacy reinforced the Germans' sense of their unique relationship with the universal Roman church.

In 1281 the German scholar and canon Alexander von Roes (*c*.1225–*c*.1300) reiterated all these ideas in a tract on the prerogatives of the Roman Empire, asserting the empire's continuing independence of the papacy and rebuffing French claims to primacy following the death of Frederick II. The empire was a universal empire, Alexander argued; it had been translated from the Romans to the Germans, who would manage it until the end of time; they alone held responsibility for the universal Christian commonwealth. These were lofty claims in the first post-Hohenstaufen decades.

The 'lesser kings' and the first Habsburg king

After Innocent IV deposed Frederick II in July 1245 the German princes rapidly marginalized his son, Conrad IV, whom they had already elected king in 1237. Their first anti-king, Henry Raspe, landgrave of Thuringia, lived only nine months. Their second, the twenty-year-old Count William of Holland (r. 1247–56), collaborated with the cities and nobles of the Rhenish League, but he was constantly distracted by the need to defend his own lands in Holland and he died in battle against the Frisians in 1256.

The first election by the six electors ended in the double appointment of Richard of Cornwall (r. 1257–72), brother of Henry III of England, and Alfonso X, king of Castile (r. 1257–72/84), who claimed the duchy of Swabia through his mother. Both were essentially interested in Italy and the imperial title. King Alfonso never even set foot in Germany. King Richard was crowned at Aachen with his wife Sanchia of Provence and spent a total of three years in Germany, but he had limited interaction with the German princes.

Following Richard's death in 1272, the electors simply ignored Alfonso's notional kingship and for the next century they opted for candidates who had a territorial base but did not threaten the electors' own interests. Each of these kings inevitably exploited his position to advance the interests of his own dynasty, but none of them was able to secure the succession of his son by having him recognized as heir to the crown before his death. Each was thus dependent on cooperating with the electors and princes and spent the early years of his reign establishing his authority.

The first was Rudolf of Habsburg. He was not a prince of the empire but the energetic and successful ruler of a spread of territories in the Aargau, Upper Alsace, and Swabia. His age—fifty-five—might also have helped his election. His main rival, King Ottokar II of Bohemia, would have been too powerful.

Once elected, Rudolf arranged marriages between his daughters and the families of all the secular electors, which turned meetings of electors into an imperial family council. He endeavoured to recover all imperial property lost since 1245 and followed Richard of Cornwall by organizing the crown properties in Swabia and Alsace into bailiwicks (*Landvogteien*) under the management of loyal counts or knights rather than ministerials. He successfully transformed many payments in kind into cash payments and renewed the privileges of the imperial cities, updating their fees. He also renewed the public peace and demanded the abolition of illegal tolls.

In 1274 Rudolf called a diet at Nuremberg and required that all fiefs should be renewed within a year and a day. King Ottokar's refusal to do this in respect of Austria and Styria—he held Bohemia and Moravia in his own right and occupied Carinthia and Carniola, today's Slovenia, without legal title—was a major challenge. In January 1275 Ottokar was outlawed; three years later he was killed in battle. His son Wenceslas II (r. 1278–1305) married Rudolf's daughter Judith and was allowed to keep Bohemia and Moravia. The duchy of Carinthia was given to Rudolf's ally Meinhard II of Goriza or Görz-Tyrol, though Carniola and the Wendish Mark were now granted to Styria. Rudolf initially retained Austria and Styria personally, which generated a substantial annual income of 18,000 marks in silver; but in 1282 he conferred them jointly on his two sons, making them, and all his successors, imperial princes.

Rudolf's attempts to turn Thuringia into a crown land after the death of Landgrave Henry the Illustrious in 1288 failed, however, though he regained some old crown property and presided over a redistribution of the landgraviate's lands among Henry's heirs, which at least re-established the rights of the crown as judge and overlord. In Burgundy, he forced the count of Savoy to return some royal property and obliged Otto IV of the Franche-Comté to pay homage.

The electors and the papacy, and the death of two sons, thwarted his plans for the succession. His remaining son, Albert, would have inherited everything. Before that was even discussed, however, Rudolf himself died aged seventy-three. Sensing that the end was near, he rode to Speyer to be buried in the cathedral alongside his Salian and Hohenstaufen predecessors, whose legacy in Germany he had done so much to rescue.

Three short-lived kings followed. Adolf of Nassau (r. 1292–8) was a minor count and essentially a creature of the archbishop of Cologne. He incurred the enmity of the archbishop of Mainz when he tried to turn Thuringia and Meissen into crown lands, was deposed, and died a month later.

The election of Albert of Habsburg (r. 1298–1308) was declared illegal by Pope Boniface VIII (r. 1295–1303), but he styled himself *rex Alemanniae* and *in regem Romanorum electus* anyway. He gained control of Thuringia and took over the vacant Bohemian throne but was murdered by one his nephews, John of Swabia (later known as John Parracida), before he could use either.

Henry of Luxemburg (r. 1308–13), thirdly, secured the Bohemian crown as a fief for his fourteen-year-old son John, for whom he arranged a marriage to the young Princess Elizabeth of Bohemia. This was as important for the future as Rudolf's acquisition of Austria in 1278. Henry VII also gained papal approval and was crowned king of Italy in Milan in January 1313, but he enraged the papacy when he marched south to reclaim the Hohenstaufen lands and titles. His death at Buonconvento south of Siena in April 1313 put paid to his ambitions, however, and effectively reduced the Italian monarchy to a loose collection of northern vassals. Many of them remained tied to the German crown until 1806.

Yet again the electors shied away from electing the obvious heir, Henry's son, John of Bohemia, fearing that he might be too powerful. Some now favoured Albert's son, Frederick the Fair, duke of Austria, who was crowned king at Frankfurt by the archbishop of Cologne. The majority, however, opted for Duke Louis of Upper Bavaria (Louis IV, r. 1314–47), who was subsequently crowned at Aachen. Frederick recognized Louis as the legitimate ruler in 1325.

Securing the pope's support proved more problematic. Though located in Avignon since 1309, having fled from unrest in Rome in 1305, and under pressure from the new Franciscan Order which demanded that the papacy emulate the poverty of Christ, Pope John XXII (r. 1316–34) still claimed primacy. When Louis intervened in Italy John excommunicated him, though in 1327 Louis nonetheless had himself crowned king of Italy and emperor by the Roman nobleman Sciarra Colonna.

The papacy's critics rallied to Louis's cause. The Parisian scholar Marsilius of Padua wrote his *Defensor Pacis* (Defender of the Peace) to defend the man whom the pope contemptuously referred to only as 'the Bavarian' and to deny the pope's role in secular government. William of Ockham, who proclaimed the independence of the emperor from the pope and denied that the church could issue decrees, also spent time at Munich. Both men influenced German theorists of empire in the 14th and 15th centuries. The electors also joined in, declaring at Rhens in 1338 that the imperial crown was not dependent on the papacy and that they had the right to select the emperor without nomination, approbation, confirmation, agreement, or authorization by the pope. The pope's implacable hostility to the king ensured that Louis enjoyed considerable support in Germany for some time.

Louis made peace with the Habsburgs in 1330 but was immediately faced with the ambitions of King John of Bohemia. Ostensibly on behalf of Louis, John had made an unauthorized expedition to Italy in 1330 and entered separate negotiations with the papacy to gain recognition for his conquests. Trouble flared up again in 1335 when both the Habsburgs and the Luxemburgs claimed the right to succeed Henry, duke of Carinthia and count of Tyrol. Hoping to acquire Tyrol for himself, Louis supported the Habsburgs, but he merely precipitated a Habsburg–Luxemburg alliance against him. Carinthia went to the Habsburgs and Tyrol to the Luxemburgs. Louis finally wrested control of Tyrol from the Luxemburgs in 1342. Three years later he also acquired Holland, Zeeland, and Hennegau on the death of William II of Holland.

Yet when Clement VI (r. 1342–52) excommunicated Louis in April 1346 the tide turned against him. Five electors now voted for the young Luxemburg heir, Charles of Moravia; only the Wittelsbach electors of the Palatinate and Brandenburg remained absent. Charles's first duty, however, was to honour a Luxemburg commitment to fight on behalf of the French king against England. The Battle of Crécy on 26 August was a humiliating defeat and King John of Bohemia died in the field, but Charles returned home as king of Bohemia. He was crowned king of Germany in November, and when Louis died on a hunting expedition in October 1347 there was no obstacle to him becoming emperor.

Charles IV, Bohemia, and the Golden Bull

Within eight years Charles IV (see Figure 5) saw off a weak anti-king, Günther von Schwarzburg, divided the Wittelsbach opposition by marrying the daughter of the count Palatine, head of the second Wittelsbach dynasty, secured his re-election and coronation at Aachen, and was crowned emperor in Rome. Unlike many predecessors, he avoided involvement in Italy and focused on the German kingdom. His kingdom of Bohemia provided the necessary economic and military resources.

5. Charles IV re-established imperial government in the empire.

Consolidating the lands of the Bohemian crown was thus a priority. Charles incorporated Upper and Lower Lusatia and the Silesian duchies and ensured that they were safeguarded against intervention by any future emperor. He persuaded the pope to establish the archbishopric of Prague, which removed Prague from the metropolitan province of Mainz and offered the prospect that all the bishoprics of the lands of the Bohemian crown might be gathered in a single province. He made Prague his capital and employed Peter Parler, one of the leading architects of the day, as chief mason of the cathedral, designer of the New Town and the Stone Bridge (now known as the Charles Bridge). The foundation of a royal university in 1348, the first university in Central Europe, underlined the significance of this flourishing city.

In Germany, Charles IV diminished the crown lands by awarding some of them to loyal allies, apparently believing that doing so would make it more difficult for the electors to find an alternative to his dynasty. He travelled energetically, particularly in Upper Germany, spending half his reign in the area between Frankfurt and Breslau and one-tenth in Nuremberg alone. He also visited Metz in

1356–7 and Lübeck in 1375, the first German monarch to do so since Barbarossa and the last until Wilhelm I visited in the 1870s.

Numerous written privileges and instructions complemented the traditional itinerary. Charles's most important law was the Golden Bull of 1356, the first written constitutional law of the German kingdom, which set out the procedure for electing an emperor and remained in force until 1806. It codified the practice that had developed since the 1250s, but it also captured the hierarchy of the empire: the seven electors would sit closest to the emperor at ceremonial feasts; the order of the electors was specified; the other estates of the realm followed them.

Charles fully understood the significance of symbolism. In Bohemia he invested heavily in the cult of St Wenceslas. He paid for a magnificent reliquary bust to house Wenceslas's remains in St Vitus Cathedral; the crown on its head was one which had been used in his own coronation. Both the sacred insignia of Bohemia and of the empire were kept in his castle and publicly displayed once a year. Charles also initiated the imperial Christmas ceremony when in 1347, sword in hand, he read from St Luke's Gospel at Christmas Mass: 'there went out a decree from Caesar Augustus, that the entire world should be taxed'.

None of this, however, could guarantee lasting success. His son was crowned king of Bohemia in 1363 and of Germany in 1376, but Charles's plans to acquire Brandenburg and to promote the territorial ambitions of his brother in Luxemburg, Brabant, and Limburg galvanized a formidable alliance of princes against him. When he imposed taxes on the Swabia cities to pay for Brandenburg they too resisted and in 1376 fourteen cities formed a league against him. These events destabilized his rule before he died in 1378 and they cast a shadow over the start of his son's reign.

The early years of Charles IV's reign coincided with the Great Plague, which swept the empire in 1349–52, reducing its population by about a third. There were repeated outbreaks until about 1400 and the population did not reach the pre-plague level again until about 1450. Many survivors took refuge in the towns; about 25 per cent of all rural settlements were abandoned. The following decades were characterized by frequent peasant uprisings and lawlessness among impoverished minor nobles who turned to feuding for the income that their estates no longer generated. The imperial cities responded best to the crisis, developing political elites, new approaches to government, and engagement in economic activity. Some princes, however, also managed to intensify their hold over their lands by introducing the system of administrative districts (*Ämter*) under the supervision of bailiffs (*Amtmänner*) which became standard for the German territories.

The empire, by contrast, struggled to rise to the challenges of government in the late 14th century. These included anxiety about public order in Germany and the uncertainty generated by the great papal schism in 1378–1415. This resulted from the double election after Gregory XI's return from Avignon in 1377. Following his death in 1378 the Roman nobles demanded an Italian pope and elected Urban VI (r. 1378–89), who proved an autocratic pontiff; the opposition elected Clement VII (r. 1378–94), who immediately returned to Avignon. The schism continued; indeed between 1409 and 1415 three rival popes ruled simultaneously.

The growing demand in Germany that these problems be addressed underlined the inadequacy of Charles's son, Wenceslas I. When Wenceslas was imprisoned by fractious Bohemian nobles in 1394, the electors immediately deemed the throne to be vacant and deposed him in 1400. He simply continued as king of Bohemia until his death in 1419. But the election of Rupert of the Palatinate (head of the second Wittelsbach dynasty in the empire) achieved little except to germinate the opposition that paralysed his kingship by the time of his death in 1410.

Sigismund and the reform of church and empire

The Luxemburg dynasty offered the only serious candidates. A small faction elected Charles IV's son Sigismund (r. 1410–37). A larger group insisted on Sigismund's cousin Jobst of Moravia, though he died the following year. Sigismund was promptly re-elected but it was three years before he came to Germany for his coronation at Aachen in 1414, which indicates the difficulty of the first decade of his rule. Bohemia remained in the hands of his stepbrother Wenceslas. Sigismund had been king of Hungary since 1387, which also gave him Dalmatia, Croatia, Serbia, and Bulgaria. But it brought him few resources, perennial problems of fierce regional opposition, and the need to repel occupying Turkish forces. The claim made by Ladislaus of Naples to the Hungarian throne in 1403 tied Sigismund down in Italy and engulfed him in prolonged conflict with Venice, to which Ladislaus had sold his rights to Dalmatia. Even when Sigismund finally inherited Bohemia in 1419, he encountered noble opposition and the prolonged Hussite insurrection, an anticlerical religious reform movement headed by Jan Hus which inflamed the Czech population from 1402. Sigismund was not recognized as king for seventeen years.

In Germany Sigismund had virtually no property—even Luxemburg was pledged—and his long absences made him reliant on a small number of confidants. His first visit to Germany for his coronation seemed promising. He travelled from Aachen to Constance to preside over key sessions at the church council that deliberated there from 1414 to 1418. This resolved the schism by deposing two popes, forcing one to resign, and electing Martin V (r. 1417–31). It also asserted the authority of the church council and resolved that the councils should be held at regular intervals, though both resolutions later led to conflict. Above all the attempt to deal with heresy failed, and the trial and execution of Hus in 1415 merely prolonged the Hussite insurgency for another two decades.

The church councils of Pavia (1423–4) and Basle (1431–49) plunged the church into a bitter struggle between papacy and council. Proposals for reforming the empire, made at diets in 1414 and 1417, led nowhere, which generated further demands for a general review. A renewed Hussite offensive in 1425 initiated another decade of conflict which only ended with a peace agreed at Prague in 1435. In the 1430s, furthermore, the duchy of Burgundy, which also owned Brabant, Limburg, Holland, Zeeland, and Hennegau, challenged imperial authority in the north-west. Constant unrest in Hungary also impeded Sigismund's ability to provide effective leadership.

Sigismund was crowned emperor in Rome in 1433 but he made no impact on Italy. Perhaps his greatest legacy to the empire was that he married his daughter Elizabeth to the Habsburg Duke Albert of Austria. Following Sigismund's death in 1437, Albert was crowned king of Hungary and Bohemia and elected king of the Romans, though he died in battle against the Turks in October 1439 before he could be crowned emperor.

Alongside establishing a Habsburg succession, Sigismund's reign was significant for four other developments. First, in response to the Hussite threat Sigismund asked the diet at Nuremberg in 1422 to provide regular contingents to be supplied by all members of the empire rather than just the forces that emperors had formerly requested as feudal overlords. That raised the question of who exactly was a member and prompted the compilation of a register, later known as the *Reichsmatrikel*. In 1427, in response to a renewed Turkish offensive against Hungary, Sigismund requested the first ever general money tax in Germany, which was agreed but ineffective because there was no mechanism for collecting it.

Second, the electors again took matters into their own hands by forming an association at Bingen, though differences between them prevented them actually deposing Sigismund as they had done Wenceslas in 1399. Yet their association further strengthened their sense of being the empire's ruling elite. The Hussite crises also contributed to the growing significance of the electors of Brandenburg and Saxony since both had lands on or near the front line. The fact that they ruled over large and continuous territories while the Rhineland electorates were fragmented reinforced their importance over the next two centuries.

Third, the princes themselves began to hold assemblies in the emperor's absence, which was a significant step in the emergence of the imperial diet or Reichstag in 1495. The term *curia* formerly used to describe assemblies of nobles was now replaced by the word *dieta* or *Tag* (assembly).

Finally, the widening perception of the need for change led to the emergence of a significant reform literature. The most popular was the *Reformatio Sigismundi* of the late 1430s. The emperor did not in fact write this German text, but he had contributed to the debate by putting forward a sixteen-point text for discussion at the diet of 1437 at Eger.

Heroic survival: the long reign of Frederick III

Since Sigismund's heir Albert left only an infant son, Ladislaus Posthumous, born in February 1440 a few months after his father's death, the electors turned to the infant's uncle and guardian (and eventual heir, for he died childless in 1457), Duke Frederick of Styria, who was elected in 1440 and crowned king at Aachen in 1442 (r. 1440–93). Frederick's position was initially as weak as that of his two predecessors. He shared his claim to Styria, Carinthia, and Carniola with his younger brother Albert VI and only gained control on Albert's death. Even then the nobility resisted Frederick's constant demands for money and there was a serious uprising between 1469 and 1471. Frederick's joint regency with Albert VI and his cousin Sigismund of Tyrol in Upper and Lower Austria also gave rise to continuous friction.

In Bohemia and Hungary the nobles openly challenged the emperor's regency on behalf of Ladislaus. In Bohemia, George Podiebrad became king in 1458. Wladislas III of Poland claimed the Hungarian throne in 1440 supported by the rebel noble John Hunyadi, and in 1458 Frederick was forced to accept the kingship of Hunyadi's son Matthias Corvinus. Things were no better in Luxemburg, another part of Ladislaus's inheritance: Philip the Good of Burgundy annexed it in 1443. In Tyrol, where Frederick was initially regent for his cousin Sigismund, his appeal to France for help in a dispute with the Swiss resulted in French mercenaries invading Lorraine, the Sundgau, and southern Alsace in 1444–5.

All this left little time for governing the empire. Frederick was absent for twenty-seven years from 1444. He left his capital, Graz, for the first time for his coronation in Rome in March 1452 and even then he had to hurry back to deal with a serious noble uprising.

Other threats soon emerged. In 1453 Constantinople fell, raising fears that the Ottomans would invade Hungary and Austria and beyond. Ottoman forces attacked Carniola in 1469 and shortly afterwards Styria. Soon the Turkish menace was replaced by a Hungarian threat when Matthias Corvinus occupied Lower Austria by 1487. In the west meanwhile there was constant pressure from Charles the Bold of Burgundy (r. 1433–77) and growing French aggression, which continued until the Peace of Senlis in 1493. Meanwhile serious unrest in the territories acquired by the marriage of Frederick's son Maximilian with the Burgundian heiress Maria was only resolved in 1488.

What may seem like a litany of problems and failures was actually a story of heroic survival. Over fifty-four years—the longest reign of any emperor—Frederick was notable for his persistence. He was convinced of the value and destiny of his dynasty. Like his father, he had always used the title of archduke and he twice confirmed the validity of the *Privilegium maius*, the document forged by Duke Rudolf IV in 1359 to claim special privileges for the

Habsburgs, including the administration of justice without appeal to the emperor and the title of an archduke Palatine.

Frederick's prolonged absences from the empire led later historians to bestow on him the scornful title of *Reichserzschlafmütze* (Arch-Sleepyhead of the Holy Roman Empire), yet his reign was exceptionally important. His 1442 peace ordinance, the *Reformatio Friderici*, was designed to be perpetual and declared feuds to be legitimate only after a failed judicial process. It was also the first such ordinance that was widely disseminated throughout the empire. In 1448 he brokered the Vienna Concordat, which, although never promulgated as an imperial law, governed the relationship between empire and papacy until 1806. In the empire he made the most of his judicial powers by transferring the administration of justice from the old Hofgericht (aulic court) to a reformed Kammergericht which soon attracted cases from many parts of the empire. Some princes even believed that the emperor was becoming too powerful.

Diets continued in Frederick's absence. They discussed issues that had been raised repeatedly since the 1430s, notably an absolute prohibition of feuds and the establishment of regional enforcement associations. Repeatedly, however, the emperor (through his representatives), the princes, and the cities clashed over how these measures might be implemented. Between 1454 and 1467, prompted by the Turkish threat, they deliberated on the mobilization of money and men in times of danger and on the role of the electors in the empire's government. The only outcome was another *Landfrieden* or domestic peace in 1467 which fully banned feuding for the first time. Even another Turkish threat in the late 1460s, which moved Frederick to preside in person at the Regensburg 'Christian diet' in 1471, resulted only in the creation of a force too small to make any difference. The real innovation in 1471 was that the various estates consulted in groups before bringing their views to the plenary sessions, which became the standard procedure of the early modern imperial diet.

Meanwhile the threat of lawlessness in southern Germany and of Bavarian expansionism was countered by imperial support for the formation of the Swabian League of princes and cities, the largest of all the traditional leagues designed to maintain the peace in the absence of any formal peacekeeping mechanisms.

In his entreaties to the princes and cities to defend the empire against its enemies, Frederick appealed for the first time to the 'German nation'. The sense of the term was ambiguous for it could mean 'German estates' as well as 'ethnic nation'. Others still preferred older terms such as 'lands of the German tongue' or the 'German lands'. All were used with increasing frequency in the second half of the 15th century. The psychological impact of the Turkish threat was crucial: the Burgundians and the French were referred to as the 'Turk in the West'. Growing dissatisfaction with the papacy, manifest in long lists of complaints or *Gravamina Germanicae nationis* against Rome presented at diets from 1456, also reinforced the desire for reform and the rhetoric of nationhood which Humanist scholars, inspired by the publication in 1473/4 of Tacitus' recently rediscovered *Germania*, helped disseminate.

Matters came to a head when Matthias Corvinus took Vienna in 1485. Fearing that Corvinus would now seek the imperial crown, Frederick pushed successfully for the election of his son Maximilian at Frankfurt in 1486, the first son elected during the lifetime of his father for over a century. The princes also agreed to a general tax to fund troops to defend the empire against Hungary and to renewal of the internal peace and its outright ban on feuds. But at the same time they demanded greater participation in the administration of justice. In fact little money was paid and the issues were simply carried forward.

In 1488 Frederick handed over active government to his son Maximilian. The new reign began with ambitious plans to restore the empire to its former glory and to use the Burgundian and Austrian territories to dominate it as no emperor had done before. Maximilian failed, but his negotiations with the German estates resulted in a new constitutional deal which transformed the empire.

Chapter 4

The early modern empire (1): from Maximilian I to the Thirty Years War

New imperial visions and social and intellectual ferment

No emperor was more image-conscious than Maximilian I (r. 1493–1519). He may well have authored the epic poem *Theuerdanck*, a fictionalized account of his courtship of and betrothal to Maria of Burgundy written as the story of a knight's quest. He certainly commissioned his secretary to write *The White King*, which recorded his life until 1513, and to compile *Freydal*, a pictorial record of his jousts and associated costume festivals. All three works combined elements of medieval literary tradition with the rich cultural imagination of the 15th-century Burgundian court. The first was also published in printed form and each reflected Maximilian's affinity with the new learning of Humanism. Maximilian surrounded himself with writers such as Conrad Celtis who promoted his image and extolled his ancient lineage. He was fascinated by the potential of the new print media as well as the propagandistic power of literature and art.

Maximilian's reign was characterized by a mixture of old and new. He wanted to restore the empire and reclaim lost lands and prerogatives. He failed to achieve this, but his negotiations with the German estates brought major reforms. It remained a feudal society, in which the princes owed allegiance to the emperor, but it now gained more elements of a written constitution. Subsequently, the empire acquired a more extensive body of constitutional law than any other early modern European monarchy.

The beginnings of this remarkable transformation originated in the general sense of uncertainty that characterized the lands of the Holy Roman Empire around 1500. Discussion of 'reform' (*reformatio*) was widespread. This usually referred to the state of the empire and of the church, but 'reform' also denoted something much broader. Many commentators were convinced that the whole world was out of joint: God's natural order had been subverted and the world was ruled by the devil; reform was essential if mankind was to be redeemed. Many advocated returning to a just and natural state of things: the empire should once more be as it had been under the Staufer, the church as it had been in the time of the Apostles.

It is difficult to identify precisely the sources of these anxieties. Similar sentiments were expressed elsewhere in Europe but they assumed a particular intensity in the German lands. For the Germans believed that they held a particular responsibility for reform of the empire and of the church. This had been discussed ever since the later 14th century. The debate had stalled around 1440 but then gathered pace again amid rising concern about increasing lawlessness and insecurity.

Some historians speak of a general crisis of German society in the early 16th century. The evidence is far from clear. Steady growth characterized the period after 1470 as the population recovered from the Black Death and prices began to rise. The hugely profitable mining industry boomed in many parts of Middle and Upper Germany, stimulating numerous other crafts and trades. Population growth and prosperity created demand for foodstuffs and fostered the development of new rural industries in many areas, especially in textiles.

Many profited from these developments but others lost out. Landlords seized the opportunity to make profits on foodstuffs; peasants were obliged to work harder and resented not being able to market their produce themselves. Some cities and towns prospered; others stagnated or declined because they were distant from key resources or were bypassed by new trading and commercial routes. Owners of shares in mines reaped rich rewards, but the miners resented long hours, harsh conditions, and low wages. Rural industry benefited many but it also divided the haves and have-nots, the rural operatives and urban managers or brokers. It also frequently placed pressure on the traditional urban guilds.

Where territorial rulers sought to strengthen their hold on their lands, peasants were frequently subjected to higher taxation or denied access to communal forests or the right to hunt and fish. Formerly free knights found themselves turned into subjects of powerful neighbouring princes. Where the landlord or prince was also a cleric—an abbot or a bishop—the sense of grievance was often aggravated by accusations that the servants of the church were the greatest oppressors of their fellow men.

Complaints against the church had been articulated in *gravamina* (catalogues of grievances) at imperial diets since the early 15th century. Common themes were the corruption of Rome and the papacy's taxation of the laity. The latter was especially heavy in Germany because of the absence of a central authority to resist it. It was well known that the money was used for worldly purposes. Furthermore, the growing practice of selling indulgences, which some practitioners turned into a major commercial enterprise, seemed to underline Rome's rapacity and its betrayal of Christian principles.

Two other developments swelled the ranks of those critical of the church. First, Benedictine and Augustinian renewal movements from the early 15th century and the spread of the ideas of the *Devotio Moderna*, a series of lay communities founded at Deventer in 1374, disseminated new practices of piety. These included cults of saints and their shrines, the endowment of masses, and pilgrimage movements. Criticism of the church escalated, as did communal involvement in its affairs, especially the appointment of pastors or the management of church funds.

Second, the development of Humanism created a new intellectual framework for opposition to Rome and for communal Christianity. The publication of Tacitus' *Germania* in Nuremberg in 1473–4, from an ancient manuscript rediscovered in the 1420s and taken to Italy around 1455, was perfect material for the Humanist agenda of a return to origins, and it gave further ammunition to critics of the papacy. Papal apologists had claimed that Tacitus' history showed how much the primitive Germans owed to Rome. The German Humanists countered that the Germans were an indigenous people, whose ancestry long pre-dated the Romans or even the Greeks: Rome had merely exploited them and limited their natural freedom. Liberation from Rome became an obsession for some Humanists and their writings provided powerful arguments for reform of empire and church.

The clamour of voices demanding change was united, moreover, as no movement had been previously, by the new medium of print. The invention of movable types by Johannes Gutenberg in Mainz around 1439 rapidly revolutionized communications. Literacy was still confined to a minority but complex ideas were popularized in pamphlets and broadsheets, many of them illustrated for greater effect. The real print revolution only exploded in the 1520s, but the printing of Bibles and devotional literature for the common man flourished from the 1470s. Indeed, the bulk of what was printed was in one way or another religious.

Imperial reforms around 1500

The first reform initiatives were directed at the empire. Maximilian I's accession in 1493 brought a new energy to imperial politics. Owing to his father's efforts, Maximilian was heir to lands in Burgundy as well as in Austria. He was ambitious to consolidate these and to regain for his dynasty the crowns of Bohemia and Hungary lost by Frederick III following Ladislaus Posthumous's death in 1457.

Maximilian also aspired to restore what the empire had lost in Italy and in Provence, the old kingdom of Burgundy. His task was made more difficult by French ambitions in Milan and Naples and by Aragonese (later, Castilian) control of Sicily. The situation was further complicated by the involvement of the powerful Republic of Venice, sometimes in alliance with the papacy, determined to thwart Maximilian's ambition to acquire Goriza (Görz). Venice even blocked Maximilian's progress to Rome in 1507, which prevented his coronation as emperor and resulted in him assuming the title of Elected Roman Emperor. Further north, Swiss forces had obliged him to conclude the Peace of Basle in 1499, and suspicion of Habsburg territorial ambitions in both south-western Germany and western Austria led the Old Swiss Confederacy to leave the empire in 1505. This secession was formally recognized by the Peace of Westphalia in 1648.

Consolidating his lands on the western and the eastern periphery of the empire and reconquering lost territory exceeded Maximilian's resources. In 1495 he asked the German princes and cities for money and men. At an imperial diet in Worms in 1495 the German estates had other ideas. They agreed to contribute to the defence of the empire from attack by the Ottomans and France but not to the reconquest of Italy.

The German estates were furthermore unwilling to provide either men or money under Maximilian's command: in emergencies they would provide armed forces that remained under their own control. They also rejected Maximilian's plans to develop a central imperial government and introduce an imperial tax. Their own proposals for the reform of the empire aimed to ensure greater stability and security and to preserve their traditional liberties. The empire would remain an elective monarchy; the princes and cities would continue to enjoy governmental authority over their own territories; they would act collectively to guarantee the domestic peace.

Several key agreements were reached at Worms. The Perpetual Peace outlawed all troublemakers. The Reichskammergericht, or imperial chamber court, was instituted to resolve all domestic disputes, including those between rulers and their subjects. The imperial diet, which now called itself 'Reichstag' for the first time, was designated as sovereign, a place where law was made jointly by 'Kaiser und Reich'. A basic tax, the 'gemeiner Pfennig' (common penny), was agreed to finance the Reichskammergericht.

The princes scuppered a plan for a central administrative body and subsequent diets established circles (*Kreise*) or regional associations of territories to enforce the judgments of the Reichskammergericht, to implement laws agreed jointly between emperor and estates, and organize periodic mobilizations of men and money. These regional institutions succeeded because they were unambiguously under the control of the estates. The determination of the estates to keep the crown within the bounds of what had been agreed in 1495–1500 was further reinforced in 1519 when they resolved that Charles V should sign an electoral capitulation (*Wahlkapitulation*) before his coronation. All subsequent emperors signed such a capitulation, which recent scholars view as a key constitutional document.

Maximilian's wings had been clipped. While he was able to defend the German kingdom, his campaigns in Italy and Provence failed and simply plunged him into hopeless debt. By the time he died in 1519, he owed more than six million gulden. Overall, the estates emerged as the winners of the renegotiation of the polity around 1500. That was reflected in the new title they now insisted on for the empire: no longer the Holy Roman Empire but the Holy Roman Empire of the German Nation.

The Reformation and the empire

Meanwhile a movement had developed in Thuringia that would fundamentally transform the religious landscape, reinforce the new constitutional order, and shape the course of German history for the next three centuries. Martin Luther's challenge to the practice of indulgences in October 1517 marked the turning point in a protracted personal spiritual odyssey played out amid the diverse religious currents of the time. Luther's emphasis on the sufficiency of the faith of the individual Christian implicitly challenged the role of the church and inspired many to reject it altogether, arguing that Christians needed neither popes nor bishops, but simply well-organized and sincere Christian communities.

When Rome itself condemned Luther, he broadened his appeal to the German nation. Many viewed him as a figurehead who might redress their own grievances against the church. Luther rejected the pope's demand that he recant his heretical views and publicly incinerated the printed version of the papal bull together with volumes of canon law in front of the town gate in Wittenberg. He became a national hero when he appeared before the emperor at the imperial diet in April 1521 and publicly stood by his views, which obliged the emperor to carry out his threat to outlaw him.

While the emperor and princes argued over how to proceed, Luther's ideas, now widely known through the dissemination of his three great Reformation tracts of 1520, spawned a prolific popular movement. The new religious teaching was taken up enthusiastically by urban and rural communities and by discontents everywhere who believed that the new interpretation of the gospels provided theological sanction for their complaints. Many went much further than Luther ever intended, aspiring to overturn the existing order to prepare for the kingdom of God on earth. Before long numerous towns and cities had embraced the Reformation; an uprising of knights had attempted to halt the growth of territorial states in the Upper Rhineland, Swabia, and Franconia; and an uprising of peasants in 1524–5 culminated in a declaration of war on lords and princes led by Luther's former colleague, Thomas Müntzer.

The movement encountered few obstacles. Maximilian I's death in January 1519 initiated an eighteen-month interregnum. The electors had decided on Maximilian's grandson Charles at the end of June 1519 but he was unable to travel to Germany to be crowned until October 1520. He only summoned his first diet the following spring.

This slow beginning reflected the complexity of Charles V's situation, which, ironically, resulted from the position of immense power that he occupied. Where Maximilian had a dual focus on both the east and the west, Charles (see Figure 6) was decidedly western. Born in Ghent and educated in Brussels, he became duke of Burgundy in 1515 and inherited the Spanish crown (with Naples, Sicily, Sardinia, and the Spanish colonies in the Americas and Asia) from his maternal grandfather in 1516. Acquiring the German imperial crown in 1519 seemed to open up the prospect of a new world empire. Yet controlling its various component parts was never easy. Facing rebellion in Spain, his most important source of income, and threats from France in Italy and from the Ottomans in the Mediterranean, Charles was absent from Germany between 1522 and 1530 (and again between 1532 and 1540).

These absences limited Charles's authority in Germany. His decision to outlaw Luther was undermined by the elector of Saxony's determination to protect his subject. Furthermore, some princes

6. Charles V by Holbein; his grand imperial vision foundered on the opposition of the German princes.

actively sympathized with the new teaching and even promoted it in the interests of the better management of the parishes and other church institutions in their lands. Above all, the German estates were united in their opposition to any unilateral action by the emperor. They soon concluded that nothing should be done until a general council of the church, or at least a German church council, had discussed the *gravamina* of the German nation.

Charles struggled to manage these issues from a distance. He appointed his brother Ferdinand, who had inherited Maximilian's Austrian lands, as his regent in Germany, but he was rarely willing to allow him much discretion. He was slow to comply with Maximilian's will which gave Ferdinand ownership of the Austrian territories. He promised to secure Ferdinand's election as heir apparent but did nothing about it until 1530. Charles seemed set on frustrating his brother's ambitions. And both Charles and Ferdinand were increasingly reliant on the German estates for help with their campaigns against the Ottomans and the French. This simply strengthened the bargaining power of the German princes and cities.

They meanwhile acted to prevent the spread of anarchy. The shock of the Peasants' War in 1525 persuaded more princes that the only way to control the Lutheran movement was to embrace it. In 1526 the diet resolved that pending a national church council each ruler should follow his own conscience. It was not long before urban and territorial governments seized the opportunity to take control of the church and educational structures. In 1529 the first Protestant university was established at Marburg and higher schools were reformed or newly founded throughout the lands which embraced the new teaching. The new religion also required new artistic forms. The sacred items venerated by previous generations and the old devotional art were disposed of. By the mid-1520s, for example, what had been the largest collection of relics in the empire, amassed by Elector Frederick the Wise, had been dissolved and was rapidly replaced by an equally remarkable collection of paintings and prints by Lukas Cranach and his workshop. Similarly, new forms of worship required new church music, notably hymns, of which Luther himself contributed a significant number. The cultural competition between the territories gained an invigorating confessional dimension.

The rapid creation of urban and territorial churches soon made it impossible to agree any coherent empire-wide policy. In 1529 the diet again tried to stem the spread of Protestantism by reaffirming the Edict of Worms and by prohibiting those who had embraced the new teaching from any further innovation. Fourteen princes and cities, however, formally protested against this: they were the first to be known as 'Protestants'.

In 1530, flushed with victory against France and freshly crowned by the pope in Bologna, Charles travelled to Germany to demand that the Protestants declare their beliefs. The Protestant Augsburg Confession was countered by the Catholic *Confutatio* (refutation or confutation) and Charles ruled that the *Confutatio* should prevail. Faced with the possibility of the Edict of Worms being executed against them, the Protestants formed a defensive league at Schmalkalden. The Protestant alliance deepened during Charles's renewed absence from Germany after 1532, while Ferdinand remained dependent on the Protestants for military assistance against the Ottomans, who had besieged Vienna again in 1529.

The Peace of Augsburg

By 1540 Charles was determined to destroy Protestantism in Germany but encountered fierce opposition. His defeat in 1552 resulted in the Peace of Augsburg in 1555. This reaffirmed the constitutional principles developed in the reign of Maximilian I and precipitated Charles's abdication as emperor in favour of Ferdinand. The great dream of an empire spanning the old world and the new had collapsed. The liberties of the German nation emerged triumphant.

The Augsburg settlement extended the Perpetual Peace to matters concerning religion. Rulers, including the councils of imperial cities and even the imperial knights, were now empowered to impose their religion on their subjects. The only proviso was that they were obliged to allow dissenters the right to emigrate. Some questions were left unclear: most notably the status of those ecclesiastical territories that had already been secularized, and the rights of Protestant nobles and towns in the Catholic ecclesiastical territories. But these things only later became contentious.

The settlement made the agreements of 1495–1500 truly workable. Furthermore, after decades of uncertainty and the bitter experience of war in the 1540s, there was a general will to abide by the peace. This was evident in the attitudes of the emperors who succeeded Charles V and in the behaviour of the German princes.

Unlike Charles V, both Ferdinand I (r. 1558–64) and Maximilian II (r. 1564–76) were essentially German emperors. Charles's political vision was always European rather than German. After long years as his brother's regent in Germany, as king of Bohemia since 1526, and as designated heir to the imperial throne since 1531, Ferdinand I had more experience of the German empire than Charles. As ruler of the Austrian lands, Ferdinand was himself a prince of the empire and his position was similar to that of previous emperors who had owned lands on its south-eastern periphery.

Maximilian II was born in Vienna and had fought with Charles V in the Schmalkaldic War in 1546–8; subsequently a four-year period as stadtholder in Spain ended when the emperor was defeated in Germany. His experiences in Madrid, and his bitterness at Charles's attempt to exclude him from the succession and make his own son Philip emperor, turned him against his Spanish relatives and made him sympathetic to the position of the German princes. On his return to Vienna in 1552, he forged close bonds with leading Catholic and Protestant princes, and by the time of his succession he was well acquainted with the leading German rulers and well versed in the practices of German government and politics.

Ferdinand and Maximilian each had a deep understanding of the confessional situation and favoured those who strove for neutrality. Ferdinand I resisted the spread of Protestantism in his own lands but he saw the need to compromise and to avoid the involvement of controversial theologians in imperial politics. He repeatedly urged the papacy to reform and to consider measures such as the recognition of communion under both kinds and the relaxation of celibacy, which he believed might tempt the German Protestants to rejoin the church.

Maximilian II's religious views were so unorthodox that they almost impeded his succession. In Vienna after his return from Spain, he relished engaging with both Catholic and Protestant intellectuals from the Netherlands, Spain, and Italy. While Ferdinand also encouraged these figures as part of his conciliatory Catholic reform programme, it seems that Maximilian effectively abandoned his Catholic faith. For the sake of his inheritance, he swore solemnly that he would not leave the Church of Rome, but the papacy distrusted him and his views fostered the growth of Protestantism in his own lands. In the empire, Maximilian pursued conciliation and compromise. He was absolutely committed to the peace settlement of 1555 and to his own role as arbitrator in the empire and co-regent with the diet.

Ferdinand and Maximilian both reached out beyond the confessional divide. They maintained friendships with a wide variety of princes, which they fostered in personal meetings and an extensive correspondence. In doing so they helped adapt the traditional networks of the German higher nobility to the new circumstances of the empire after the Peace of Augsburg.

The settlement of 1555 gave a new impetus to the empire's key institutions. The diet met seven times between 1556–7 and 1582, with the emperor attending personally. The discussions and deliberations followed the procedure laid down around 1500 and codified by the imperial arch-chancellor, the elector of Mainz, in 1570. The diet debated current problems of internal peace, the organization of the circles, the state of the currency, the operations of the Reichskammergericht, and imperial taxes, notably for the various Turkish campaigns; decisions concerning religion were devolved to the urban and territorial governments. In addition, there were three meetings of the electors, a general assembly of the circles, several so-called Reichsdeputationstage (special gatherings of representatives of the estates convened to discuss a range of issues specified by the diet), as well as a number of meetings convened to discuss specific issues such as the management of the

imperial court of justice, the Reichskammergericht, and the
distribution of the burden of imperial taxes.

The circles now also developed regular assemblies and specialist
committees to deal with matters such as the regulation of the
currency. They appointed officers to lead and represent them
and officials to coordinate their business. Not every region
developed the same level of activity: those which comprised
numerous small territories, especially in Middle and Upper
Germany, tended to be the most active; where larger territories
dominated, they tended to resolve disputes and regulate other
activities engaged in by the circles elsewhere. Simultaneously
new regional organizations of imperial counts and imperial
knights now bound these groups into the empire's institutional
structure, offering them greater protection and ensuring the
security of their lands.

The Reichskammergericht was complemented after 1559 by
the emperor's own supreme court at Vienna, the Reichshofrat,
forming a pair of occasionally competing but generally
complementary supreme courts for the empire. The staffing of
the Reichskammergericht was enhanced, funding increased, and
procedures improved. The court's authority grew with its caseload
and there were only seven appeals against its judgments between
1559 and 1585.

The reformed Vienna Reichshofrat also contributed to the
pacification and 'juridification' of the empire. Some litigants
preferred it since its procedures were more flexible and
expeditious than those of the Reichskammergericht. The
Reichshofrat's custom of sending commissions to gather evidence
on the ground involved local powers in the conflict resolution
process and solved many problems by local arbitration. The old
notion that the Reichshofrat was favoured by Catholic litigants is
confounded by the fact that Protestants used it just as frequently.
Despite later claims of confessional bias, its caseload doubled

between 1580 and 1610. Both courts attracted cases from western and northern areas, as well as from the old core lands of Middle and Upper Germany, which demonstrated the growing reach of imperial justice and the contribution made by the courts to the integration of the empire.

Historians have often viewed the diet as dysfunctional and weak, and its procedures frequently puzzled contemporaries. Yet a number of key decisions made by the diet exemplified a new sense of solidarity and purpose after 1555. Its handling of both domestic and foreign issues demonstrated a high degree of rationality and practicality.

Around 1500 the German estates had made it clear that they would defend themselves but not promote purely Habsburg interests. The emperors' constant requests for money to help defend the empire against the Ottomans met with ready compliance. Indeed the sum granted in 1576 brought in some 3.7 million gulden, more than all of the Turkish levies granted under Charles V before 1555 combined.

In the early 1570s the Livonia affair clearly demonstrated the continuing significance of the distinction between German and purely Habsburg interests. Livonia did not formally belong to the Holy Roman Empire but the German estates broadly supported Ferdinand I's claim that it was part of his wider empire. Yet they did not support Maximilian II's attempts to assert his claims first against Denmark and Sweden, then against Poland-Lithuania. Traditional German historiography took this as a sign of the diet's weakness and lack of national spirit. In reality, however, the diet simply applied the same criteria as it had done in the case of Maximilian I's Italian plans around 1500. The 'recuperation' of Livonia and Maximilian's efforts to place Habsburg candidates on the Polish throne in 1573 and 1575 were simply Habsburg projects, which some princes also believed would make the emperor too powerful in the north.

The diet also refused to become involved in the Netherlands conflict which broke out in 1568. The Dutch rebels appealed for assistance against the tyrannical religious policies which Spain imposed on the Netherlands. However, even though many German nobles were personally related to William of Orange and the house of Nassau, and many counts themselves converted to Calvinism, the diet prioritized its determination to maintain the peace and stability of the empire over involvement in a potentially ruinous conflict.

Maintaining the domestic peace was another priority. The diet of 1566 provided an impressive demonstration of the common interest of both emperor and estates in peace and the effective functioning of the circles and other imperial bodies. An unprecedented levy was agreed to support the emperor's defence of the empire against the Ottomans. To deal with the instability caused since 1558 by Wilhelm von Grumbach's pursuit of his grievances against the bishops of Würzburg, the diet commissioned the elector of Saxony, under the ultimate command of the emperor, to destroy Grumbach's forces.

After a failed attempt to mediate between the two religious parties in 1556–7, the diet simply confirmed the agreements of 1555 without further discussion of the question of religious reunification. Debate over whether the elector of the Palatinate's conversion to Calvinism placed him outside the religious peace in the empire was simply avoided when the other Protestant princes swore that they recognized him as an adherent of the (Lutheran) Augsburg Confession.

In 1570 the princes once again rejected a plan to create a standing army under the emperor's command as well as permanent armouries and war chests in the circles for the emperor to draw on. Creating such an army would have compromised the constitution; some feared the empire's transformation into a centralized state. In the 1576 session of the diet, Saxony and Bavaria helped thwart a

Palatine initiative to demand formal recognition of the rights of Protestant nobles and towns in ecclesiastical territories (the *Declaratio Ferdinandea*), which the Catholics would have opposed.

New tensions

The situation deteriorated decisively in the 1580s. The death in 1586 of Elector August I of Saxony (r. 1553–86) removed the last leading member of the 'generation of 1555'. A growing number of disputes and controversies arising from the peace of 1555 created tension. The successful imposition of confessional regimes in many leading Catholic and Protestant territories by the 1580s generated a new and uncompromising approach to politics in the empire before the Thirty Years War.

The pressure of conflicts in the Netherlands and in France and the impact of news of the beginnings of a decisive Counter-Reformation policy in some of the Austrian territories aggravated the situation. The movement of Spanish troops up the Rhine on their route from Spain via Genoa to the Netherlands and their incursions in the north-west, as well as the periodic involvement of the Palatinate and others in the Protestant cause in France, unsettled German politics. Yet the majority refused to be dragged into external disputes, their solidarity reinforced by the Turkish threat, in respect of which the diet voted substantial levies in 1594, 1597–8, and 1603 (the highest levy ever agreed).

A 'mini Ice Age' that began in 1570 also contributed to a widespread sense of crisis by the 1590s. The German territories faced growing problems posed by poverty, social unrest, and peasant rebellions, and the various witch crazes after about 1580. Short-term climate change destabilized German society into the first decades of the 17th century.

Rudolf II (r. 1576–1612) did not at first deviate from the course set by Ferdinand I and Maximilian II. His Spanish education gave him the reputation of being a hard-line Catholic. Yet in 1582, he defused the potentially explosive issues thrown up by disputes over the question of Protestant worship in the Catholic imperial city of Cologne, over the demand of the Protestant administrator of the archbishopric of Magdeburg to take the Magdeburg seat in the college of princes, and over the conversion of the elector archbishop of Cologne, Gebhard Truchsess von Waldburg, to Protestantism (which ended in Waldburg's forcible deposition in 1584 and the election of a Bavarian Wittelsbach successor).

Indeed the papacy regarded Rudolf with as much suspicion as it had his predecessors. Both in Bohemia and in the empire he was as committed as Maximilian II to the idea that no single faith should predominate. His permanent withdrawal to Prague in fact brought him closer to the empire: after the partition of the Habsburg lands following the death of Ferdinand I, it was Vienna that became remote, since the Tyrol and the south-western Habsburg lands were until 1665 in the hands of a subsidiary line that consistently promoted the Counter-Reformation. Prague was much better placed for communications with north, middle, and southern Germany than Vienna, and it was well beyond the reach of Ottoman forces.

After about 1599–1600, however, many contemporaries commented on Rudolf II's withdrawal, his illness and changed state of mind, and on the increasing chaos that prevailed in his administration. He abandoned his previous advisers and turned to a new group of predominantly Catholic courtiers. He was also tormented by growing tensions within his own family, as his brother Matthias and others pressed him to reach a decision on the succession. Rudolf had several illegitimate children but he never married; his indecision over the succession was motivated to a great extent by his intense dislike of his brother.

Lack of imperial leadership inevitably exacerbated the emerging controversy between Catholic and Protestant interpretations of imperial law. Increasingly, both sides rejected the judgements of the courts in disputes which arose over the interpretation of the peace of 1555, which impaired the operation of imperial justice. In 1608, the diet itself was paralysed by these issues. Rudolf's request for a levy to finance a force of 24,000 men against the Ottomans failed. The diet was dissolved.

This impasse led directly to the formation of the Protestant Union (14 May 1608) and the Catholic League (10 July 1609). A struggle between Brandenburg and Palatinate-Neuburg over the succession to Duke Johann Wilhelm of Jülich-Cleves in March 1609 looked likely to turn into war. The involvement of the French king and Rudolf's diversion of troops intended for the Lower Rhine to threaten his brother Matthias in Upper Austria made this seem even more likely, especially as the troops plundered Prague, prompting the Bohemian estates to depose Rudolf in favour of Matthias. Rudolf's death in January 1612, however, defused the situation and allowed Matthias to secure election to the imperial throne.

Matthias (r. 1612–19) behaved perfectly correctly as emperor and actively promoted plans to bridge the confessional–political divide in the empire. Yet his pursuit of rigorous anti-Protestant policies in his own lands aggravated the bitterness and distrust generated by the recent disputes and undermined his attempt to convene a diet in 1613. But the German estates still hesitated to upset the delicate balance of powers established around 1500. In 1614 both Protestant and Catholic princes stepped back from the brink of war over Jülich-Cleves. Most wished to avoid becoming embroiled either in an international Protestant alliance or in the grand designs of the Spanish crown. Indeed, among Protestants the rhetoric of these years was not the language of war but rather that of patriotism.

The Thirty Years War

The Thirty Years War (1618–48) started with a Bohemian rebellion against Habsburg rule. When the Bohemian rebels offered the throne to the Calvinist elector of the Palatinate, Ferdinand II (r. 1619–37) responded ruthlessly and imperial forces easily crushed the uprising at the Battle of the White Mountain in November 1620, Ferdinand then pursued the elector, the 'Winter King', into Germany and transferred his electorate to Duke Maximilian of Bavaria, exercising powers that had implications for all princes and not just the Palatine outlaw. Many feared that Ferdinand intended to re-Catholicize the empire, which drew more Protestant princes into the conflict and triggered the intervention of Christian IV of Denmark (also duke of Holstein).

The success of the imperial armies by 1629 and Ferdinand's Edict of Restitution, which demanded the return of all church property secularized since 1552, galvanized the Protestant opposition. It also, however, prompted the electors, Catholics and Protestants alike, to demand the dismissal of the emperor's military supremo, Wallenstein, who they feared was making the emperor too powerful in northern Germany.

The intervention of Gustavus Adolphus of Sweden, financed by French subsidies, brought Wallenstein back on to the scene, and the Swedish king fell at Lützen in November 1632. The Swedish forces were defeated in 1634 but continuing Protestant resistance resulted in the Peace of Prague in 1635, in which Ferdinand gave up the Edict of Restitution and the princes agreed to expel all foreign troops.

Despite this, France now intervened with the twofold objective of smashing the power of Habsburg Spain, which was achieved by 1659, and toppling the Habsburg emperor, whose forces they pursued through relentless campaigns in southern Germany.

Among the German princes, however, the accession of the more conciliatory Ferdinand III (r. 1637–57) fostered a desire for peace and for a return to the 'old system'.

At the end of this protracted struggle for the preservation of 'German liberty', the Peace of Westphalia (1648), comprising the Treaty of Osnabrück for the empire and the Treaty of Münster for the wider European conflict, rebalanced the constitutional status quo negotiated in the reign of Maximilian I. In the agreement reached at Osnabrück, Calvinism was now recognized alongside Lutheranism and Catholicism as an official religion of the empire. The question of who was entitled to which property was resolved by declaring 1624 to be the baseline for ownership. The rights of Catholic, Lutheran, and Calvinist (German Reformed) minorities were secured, which effectively limited the power of the princes to determine the religion of their territories, though Protestant rulers were nonetheless affirmed as *summus episcopus* (highest bishop) of their territorial churches. The Austrian lands and Bohemia were exempted from these stipulations, which enabled the Habsburgs to enforce Catholicism with impunity after 1648. Disputes concerning confessional matters in the empire were to be resolved amicably by the diet sitting in two *corpora* (parallel sections or colleges) so that the Catholic majority could not dictate to the Protestant minority. All other disputes between individual estates of the empire would be resolved peacefully through the courts.

Imperial power was formally tied to the consent of the Reichstag (all laws were promulgated by 'Kaiser und Reich'); the princes could enter into alliances, though not against the emperor and the empire; Bavaria retained its electorate, and the Palatine electorate was restored. The treaty represented the failure of Ferdinand II's ambitions and the triumph of German liberty ('deutsche Libertät') over the German monarchy. France gained Alsace; Sweden acquired Pomerania and the secularized Archbishopric of Bremen; both became guarantors, together with the emperor, of the peace treaty and of the imperial constitution. In a separate agreement at Münster, Switzerland was formally recognized as an independent state, no longer part of the Reich. The Dutch Republic's independence of the empire was recognized de facto by its signature alongside Spain's on the Treaty of Münster.

The Treaty of Osnabrück distinguished more clearly than ever before between the German empire and the wider feudal realm of the empire that still survived in northern Italy and parts of the old kingdom of Burgundy and the southern Netherlands. Habsburg intervention in these areas took various forms: fairly direct government in the southern Netherlands; looser overlordship in Italy, where the various territories and cities still regarded the emperor as their protector and the arbiter of their disputes.

In Germany, however, the position of the Habsburgs was quite different because they were now bound by a written constitution with external guarantors. Even without France and Sweden as watchdogs, the developments in Germany between 1495 and 1648 had ensured that the threat of a strong monarchy in Germany had been banished for good.

Chapter 5

The early modern empire (2): from the Peace of Westphalia to 1806

Reconstruction and renewal

The Thirty Years War was a disaster for much of the empire. The total population may have declined from about twenty million to some sixteen or seventeen million. The worst-hit areas were Pomerania and Mecklenburg in the north-east, Thuringia and Hesse in Middle Germany, and the south-west. In Württemberg the population declined by 57 per cent and pre-war levels were only reached again by about 1750. Incessant movements of marauding troops destroyed infrastructure and agriculture. Even where material damage was limited, both civilians and governments were left with substantial debts. Many nobles who had speculated on rising prices before 1618 were all but ruined by the long downturn which the conflict precipitated; some families were still paying off the debts their predecessors had incurred at this time in the 19th century.

Yet the post-war era provided new opportunities for survivors. Population loss created demand for labour; enterprising individuals and communities revived old activities and developed new skills. Territorial administrations adopted new approaches to land management and revenue creation as they engaged in the business of reconstruction. Despite the general problem of post-war indebtedness, many princes now also began to spend lavishly on building new residences and on culture: art, music, books, and other things designed to enhance the prestige of a territory and its ruling centre. Investment in 'soft power' reflected the growing political ambitions of territories such as Bavaria, Brandenburg, Brunswick, and Saxony, but also the desire of smaller territories to survive in the new competitive atmosphere of the century after 1648. These developments all contributed to the extraordinary cultural vitality of the German lands, manifest especially in the literary, musical, and philosophical achievements of the 18th and early 19th centuries.

Using Saxe-Coburg-Gotha as its model, Veit Ludwig von Seckendorff's *German Princely State* (1655) outlined the theory and practice of government in an intensively managed and paternalistic small German territory. Seckendorff's book is often cited as evidence for the rise of absolutism in this period, yet no prince enjoyed absolute power. All were to one degree or another dependent on the cooperation of the estates of their lands: the nobles, towns, and clergy represented in the assemblies which deliberated on tax proposals and other legislation. Rulers also remained subject to the laws of the empire: *Landeshoheit* (governmental overlordship) fell short of full sovereignty. Subjects had the right of appeal to imperial courts; the emperor could and did intervene if rulers contravened the rules. After 1648 a growing number of more powerful princes became impatient with the restrictions on their power in the empire. Some aspired to become fully sovereign but they could only achieve this by assuming royal crowns outside the empire: the electors of Saxony, Brandenburg, and Hanover became kings respectively in Poland, Prussia, and Great Britain.

The empire experienced a revival after 1648. Despite the setbacks suffered during the 1640s, Ferdinand III (r. 1637–57) rebuilt his authority. He reformed the Vienna Reichshofrat which the Peace of Westphalia had formally recognized as an imperial supreme court alongside the Reichskammergericht. He presided personally over a diet at Regensburg between December 1652 and May 1654. This saw agreement on reform of the Reichskammergericht and the amelioration of the burden of war debts, though the estates again refused to agree to the formation of an imperial army, resolving instead that each prince should be able to levy taxes for his own defence and for imperial defence. Many other issues were simply deferred.

Ferdinand's prestige was sufficiently restored that he was able to secure approval for his elevation of eight counts and one imperial knight to the rank of prince, which strengthened the imperial party in the diet. He also had his son elected and crowned king of the Romans as Ferdinand IV in July 1653. The latter's sudden death a year later placed the succession in jeopardy, for his second son Leopold was a minor and remained so at his father's death in 1657. Yet again, however, and despite a fifteen-month interregnum, the absence of a plausible alternative ensured Leopold's election when he came of age in 1658 (see Figure 7). Leopold I's forty-seven-year reign fully restored the position of the Habsburgs as emperors and gave substance to the imperial framework created in 1648. His policies were carried forward by his sons Joseph I (r. 1705–11) and Charles VI (r. 1711–40).

External threats and stabilization of the empire

Three external threats to the empire helped maintain its solidarity. In 1663, first, following a dispute over Transylvania, Ottoman forces once more invaded Royal Hungary and Moravia and threatened Vienna, creating panic in southern and eastern Germany. A peace negotiated in 1664 held for twenty years but its terms generated a noble independence movement in Hungary which preoccupied Vienna until the Ottomans attacked again in 1683, besieging the city for the first time since 1529. Thereafter a protracted series of campaigns culminated in the defeat of the Ottomans in 1697, when the Habsburgs were recognized as rulers of Hungary and Transylvania. Further Hungarian opposition was quelled in 1711

Leopoldo i Erwölter Romischer Kayser
auch Zu Hungarn Unnd Hohaimb Konig,
Ertzhertzog Zu Österreich.

7. Leopold I successfully restored imperial authority after the Thirty Years War.

but another Ottoman war broke out in 1716, ending in 1718 with the Peace of Passarowitz which gave the Habsburgs the Banat, northern Serbia, and Little Wallachia, all lost again in 1739 following Charles VI's decision to join a Russian war against the Ottomans in 1737.

These Ottoman wars generated the same kind of German patriotism as those in the 16th century. The German princes raised taxes, sent troops, and, in some cases, themselves fought alongside the emperor to defend the empire from Ottoman invasion.

Second, in the west, France was initially content to manipulate anti-Habsburg sentiment in the empire by encouraging the elector of Mainz's League of the Rhine (1658–68). Following the outbreak of the French war against the Dutch Republic in 1672, Lorraine, Alsace, Trier, and the Palatinate also became targets. In 1679 the Peace of Nijmegen provided a brief respite before France began its policy of *Réunion*. This involved exploiting old feudal rights to annexe any lands in the empire that had once been dependent on the territory which was ceded to France in the Peace of Westphalia. Strasbourg was lost in 1681 and French fortresses were established on the Rhine at Freiburg and Breisach.

Hostilities were renewed during the War of the Palatine Succession (1688–97) and the War of the Spanish Succession (1701–14) which was fought out in Italy and Germany. After an interval following the death of Louis XIV in 1715, the War of the Polish Succession (1733–8) and the War of the Austrian Succession (1740–8) renewed the previous pattern of periodic attacks on the empire in the context of conflicts that did not directly concern it. Finally, a new alliance system emerged in the Seven Years War which saw France allied to Austria against Prussia and the maritime powers (Britain and the Netherlands).

French aggression also posed an internal threat because France was a natural magnet for German enemies or rivals of the Habsburgs. Between the 1660s and the 1740s, Mainz, Cologne, Brandenburg, and Bavaria, among others, all periodically sought alliances with France. Bavaria even fought on the French side in both the War of the Spanish Succession and the War of the Austrian Succession.

Third, in the north, various conflicts threatened the empire's stability. Brandenburg, which was at war with Sweden between

1674 and 1679, was particularly vulnerable but Habsburg interests in Poland were also jeopardized. The Swedish–Polish war of 1655–60 also underlined the extent of French influence in the empire since France intervened to prevent Sweden's defeat and to force Austria and Brandenburg to accept a peace. French support for Sweden and interest in the Polish crown remained constant until 1700. The Habsburgs had no direct stake in the Great Northern War between Sweden and Russia 1700–21, and for much of the time they were preoccupied by the War of the Spanish Succession anyway. Consequently, the emperor became dependent on Brandenburg and the new electorate of Hanover to take the strain of defending the empire's interests against Sweden. This underlined the growth in the secular electors' power and aspirations generally, a key feature of the period after 1648.

Leopold I's authority ultimately rested on his triumph over the existential threats posed by France and the Ottomans. Yet his effectiveness as a ruler in the empire owed much to his astute handling of both royal prerogatives and imperial politics.

Leopold bolstered his domestic support by patronage. He liberally conferred privy councillorships and honorary chamberlainships, and created new titles such as arch-marshal to the empress. He also elevated new counts and barons, and turned existing counts into princes. Marriage alliances created links with the more prominent noble families. He himself married a Palatinate-Neuburg heiress as his third wife. Three of his children were married respectively into the Bavarian Wittelsbach, the Brunswick-Lüneburg, and the Brunswick-Wolfenbüttel dynasties. Bavaria turned against the Habsburgs but the Brunswick-Lüneburg line became a key northern ally against Brandenburg, a fact recognized by the elevation of the principality as the electorate of Hanover in 1692. Brandenburg aspirations, and irritation over the creation of the Hanoverian electorate, were satisfied by Leopold's, albeit reluctant, agreement to recognize the elector as king in Prussia, a territory outside the empire. Saxon ambitions were diverted when Leopold supported the elector of Saxony's bid for the Polish throne in 1697.

Leopold also engaged in the institutions of the empire. The diet he summoned to Regensburg in January 1663 was the last in the empire's history: it remained in permanent session (the 'perpetual diet') until 1806. Initially this was because the diet failed to reach agreement on key issues but gradually it proved its utility. Leopold himself only attended for five months, but he was represented throughout by the archbishop of Salzburg as Prinzipal-Kommissar, and all important papers were sent to him in Vienna. The diet's initial priority was to formulate an electoral capitulation for all future imperial elections, which was finally done by 1711. This never became law because Charles VI did not ratify the draft, but it was regarded as an informal fundamental law nonetheless.

An attempt to resolve the question of an imperial army in the 1670s resulted in agreement on the size of the army; raising troops was devolved, as before, to the circles. While various forms of economic legislation failed, the diet's legislative record did not compare badly with other European parliaments of the time, including the English parliament.

The very fact of the continuous session came to be symbolic of the empire's unity. Furthermore, many proposals that the diet discussed but did not implement found their way into initiatives taken by the circles or the territories. At these levels there was no lack of legislation; indeed this was the start of the golden age of German territorial legislative activity.

For his part Leopold used the diet to gain information, as a way of being present in the empire, even though he only ever made five journeys into it and none north of Frankfurt. For the same reason he steadily extended the network of imperial ambassadors and residents across the whole of Germany and he even used the imperial postal service run by the Thurn und Taxis family to monitor the activities of the cities and princes covertly.

The Reichshofrat was perhaps the most important vehicle of imperial influence. The Reichskammergericht was working only intermittently owing to the delinquency of princes in paying their dues to it and to interruptions occasioned by French military activity, which in 1689 occasioned its move from Speyer to Wetzlar. The emperor's supreme court in Vienna, the Reichshofrat, meanwhile established itself as a reliable, speedy, impartial, and authoritative institution. Even Protestant princes, for example those in Thuringia, increasingly took their inner-dynastic disputes there. Admittedly, the larger territories increasingly sought blanket exemption from the court's jurisdiction—another sign of their growing aspirations to greater independence and status than the other princes—but they were obliged to institute their own high courts or appeal courts. Feuding or violent conflict resolution more or less died out; many a peasant or burgher discontent was taken to the courts rather than pursued through rebellion.

Imperial patriotism

Leopold's success is reflected in new forms of imperial patriotism. Plans for the empire's future development proliferated from the 1680s. These included schemes for the reconciliation of the Christian churches, ideas for institutional reform, economic development and legal codification, and proposals for imperial academies of arts, sciences, or language. One figure who appeared repeatedly in such discussions was the philosopher and polymath Gottfried Wilhelm Leibniz, who worked initially for the elector of Mainz and then for the duke of Brunswick-Lüneburg, later elector of Hanover. No German intellectual was better networked than he was: he had over a thousand correspondents in 169 locations in Europe. His range of contacts in the empire was unrivalled and he can stand for the interconnectedness of German intellectuals, mainly through the roughly thirty-five universities. The sense of a

German academic/scientific community was further reinforced by a flourishing book trade and by the appearance of the first academic journals such as the *Acta Eruditorum* (*Philosophical Transactions*), founded at Leipzig in 1682 and dedicated to publishing original articles in the natural sciences and reviewing books from all over Europe.

Almost none of Leibniz's projects bore fruit, and the first German academy of arts and sciences was founded in 1700 in Berlin not in Vienna. Yet enthusiasm for the empire and thinking about schemes for its improvement continued well into the 18th century. One reason for the failure of Vienna-based projects may well have been that following the completion of the Leopoldine Wing of the Hofburg around 1680, Leopold built virtually nothing. The Vienna court remained centred on the 13th-century core of the castle residence which had last been modernized in the mid-16th century. To some extent that was itself programmatic: while other German dynasties and the noble families from the Habsburg lands and the empire who retained residences in Vienna built themselves new palaces, Leopold proclaimed the antiquity and continuity of his own.

Leopold I's two sons, Joseph I (r. 1705–11) and Charles VI (r. 1711–40), were more active builders. Joseph set about designing a summer palace at Schönbrunn; Charles oversaw its completion and added several grand extensions to the Hofburg, as well as the magnificent St Charles's Church (Karlskirche) in Vienna (1716–39) along with the unfinished project of transforming the abbey at Klosterneuburg into an Austrian Escorial (1723–40). These enterprises created an 'imperial style' that was widely emulated by princes in the empire. Brandenburg-Prussia and Saxony-Poland developed their own distinctive styles. Bavaria's hostility to the Habsburgs led to flirtations with French style. But among the Catholic nobility and the ecclesiastical rulers the imperial style flourished, and even some Protestant princes began to incorporate an imperial hall (*Kaisersaal*) in their residences. These magnificent halls were richly decorated with wall and ceiling paintings and statues, conveying allegorical images that underlined both the majesty of the emperor and the status of the local rulers.

The reign of Charles VI saw two other manifestations of confidence in the empire. In 1726 Johann Christoph Gottsched took over what became the Deutsche Gesellschaft in Leipzig and used it to propagate his ideas for the reform of the German language and its literature, for which he initially hoped for sponsorship from the court at Dresden before turning to Vienna in 1738. As early as 1727 he had written an ode 'In Praise of Germany' which eulogized Charles VI as the ruler of the 'new Rome'. Vienna ultimately disappointed him but his faith in Germany remained undimmed, and his literary reform proposals remained influential until the reaction of young writers against them in the 1750s marked the starting point of modern German literature.

The same period also saw a proliferation of writing about the empire: attempts to define the relationship between territories and empire, the nature of the empire, and its unique multi-level institutions and complex legal system which protected both the 'German liberty' of the princes and the rights of individuals. The most comprehensive compilation of German law was the fifty-three-volume *Teutsches Staatsrecht* (*German Public Law*, 1737–54) by the Württemberg official Johann Jacob Moser (1701–87). This monumental work started from the assumption that the empire could only be understood historically and gave a detailed account of its public law as it related to everyone from the emperor down to the peasantry. Like other writers, Moser saw the empire as a unique system which had many oddities but which cohered nonetheless.

New challenges after Leopold I

Alongside these important developments, which reinforced the German identity of the empire, Joseph I and Charles VI enjoyed mixed fortunes. Joseph I died aged thirty-one after barely six years on the throne. During that time he devoted major resources to holding on to Italy in the later stages of the War of the Spanish Succession, which he regarded as an imperial mission even if the German princes thought little of it. He also launched a reform of the judicial system, though this failed.

His brother Charles was initially a reluctant emperor, remaining deeply attached to his Spanish kingdom which he never saw again after 1711: 'Barcelona' was his dying word in 1740. Yet he soon embraced his new role. He revived the symbolism and imagery of his namesake Charles V. He initiated serious attempts to revive imperial rights and revenues. His administrative reforms in Vienna finally separated imperial from Austrian affairs, which upset the imperial vice-chancellor who felt that his role was being downgraded. But neither Charles nor his officials saw the two realms as mutually exclusive, and losing the empire would have been a huge blow to Austria. His execution of imperial justice was energetic and he intervened effectively in episcopal elections and in Mecklenburg where he deposed a tyrannical duke. If anything, Charles proved far too active an emperor for some: as early as 1716 Frederick William I of Brandenburg-Prussia (r. 1713–40) complained that 'he wants to subjugate us all and make himself sovereign'.

Charles proved powerless, however, to solve two major problems. The first was the increasingly confrontational behaviour of Brandenburg-Prussia. This resulted from the Catholic elector Palatine's attempts to exploit the terms of the Peace of Rijswijk to re-Catholicize his territory. The peace appeared to allow Catholics rights of worship wherever they had been permitted during the French occupation between 1688 and 1697. The diet failed to broker a solution; some Protestants threatened war. Finally, the elector backed down, the Protestants shied away from violence, and the emperor retained his authority.

The whole affair seemed to show that the underlying tension between Protestants and Catholics remained strong. And, while Saxony had traditionally led the Protestant cause, that role was now assumed by Brandenburg-Prussia. Saxony formally retained the chair of the Protestant Corpus in the diet at Regensburg, but the Saxon elector's conversion to Catholicism in order to take up the Polish crown undermined Saxony's position in the empire. Hanover also played a key role in supporting the rights of Protestants in the Palatinate, but its electors were increasingly preoccupied with Great Britain rather than with the empire. Brandenburg, distrusted and feared even by many of its natural allies in the empire, made the most of the situation. It had been obliged to develop a strong army by the threats it faced in the Thirty Years War and in the northern wars that followed; it was now the only German territory that could pose a credible military threat to Austria.

The second problem was the succession. Charles had four children but only his two daughters survived infancy. Joseph I had also only left two daughters. At a time when many German dynasties were adopting primogeniture it was only natural that the Habsburgs should follow suit. What Charles proposed was rather different: female succession, the retention of all imperial fiefdoms, and a guarantee by the empire of Habsburg possessions outside it. One other thing was clear, however: Charles's daughter Maria Theresa could not inherit the imperial throne; some princes even worried that agreeing to the Pragmatic Sanction would predetermine the imperial succession in favour of a future husband, provided he was a German.

In the event, Francis Stephen of Lorraine, whom Maria Theresa married in 1736, was not sufficiently powerful to be a serious candidate on Charles VI's death in 1740, even though he had exchanged Lorraine for the Grand Duchy of Tuscany in 1737. After a thirteen-month interregnum the elector of Bavaria, Charles Albert, was chosen, a man qualified by nothing more than the fact that two of his ancestors had held the imperial title in the Middle Ages.

Those who voted for Charles VII (r. 1742–5) with misgivings were soon proved right. He was chronically short of money. Since he inherited his electorate in 1726 he had been dependent on French subsidies, which continued when he was emperor. Politically and militarily, he was dependent on Prussian support. Austrian forces occupied Bavaria two days after his coronation at Frankfurt and, apart from a brief period in 1744, Charles was effectively stranded in Frankfurt. His claims to Bohemia and the Austrian lands were simply laughable in view of the fact that his army had been all but destroyed in the battle for Belgrade in 1739.

Even establishing a government—an imperial chancellery or a new Reichshofrat—proved difficult, not least because the Austrians were so slow to hand over the imperial archive that it had still not arrived in Frankfurt by the time Charles died on 20 January 1745. By then he had alienated most of his remaining supporters by taking seriously a Prussian plan to support his imperial reign by turning a series of south German bishoprics and imperial cities into crown properties.

The Bavarian experiment was a disaster. From the start it had been overshadowed by more important events initiated by the new Prussian king, Frederick II, later known as Frederick the Great (r. 1740–86). His succession coincided with the death of Charles VI. While other dynasties made claims on Habsburg lands, Frederick was the only one who acted on them by sending an army of 30,000 men into Silesia in December 1740. In three wars—1740–2, 1744–5, and 1756–63—Austria failed to recover the territory. In the first two conflicts France also became involved, supporting Bavarian and Saxon territorial claims against the Habsburgs. Prussia alone achieved its war aims: the Peace of Dresden in December 1745 confirmed Prussian ownership of Silesia.

Renewal under Habsburg-Lorraine

Although it sealed Austria's loss of Silesia, the Peace of Dresden also presaged the return of the Habsburgs. Following the death of Charles VII the electors recognized that there was no real alternative to Francis Stephen of Lorraine; even the Prussian king assented to his election as Francis I (r. 1745–65). However, Berlin then did all it could to impede the re-establishment of Habsburg authority in the empire. The spread of Brandenburg territories across north Germany meant that Frederick the Great (r. 1740–86) was represented in three imperial circles and he blocked Habsburg wishes in each. His own marriage to Elisabeth Christine of Brunswick-Wolfenbüttel-Bevern was a disaster but he paid close attention to the unions of his eight siblings, using them to forge alliances throughout central and northern Germany. He also seized every opportunity to intervene as protector of Protestants in south-west and Middle Germany.

This all proved advantageous during the last war for Silesia, 1756–63 (the Seven Years War), for it served at least to mitigate opposition to him. This conflict was part of a wider confrontation in which a new Franco-Austrian-Russian alliance stood against a Protestant British-Dutch-Prussian alliance. The main issue for most of those involved was the struggle between Britain and France for control of the Atlantic colonies. Yet Austria used its new alliance with France to launch another attempt to regain Silesia.

Frederick's occupation of Saxony prompted the diet to outlaw him. Prussian propaganda, and later Prussian-German historians, eulogized the king for standing up yet again for the Protestant cause and for heroic military victories. In fact Frederick's victories were few and far between and he was lucky to survive the war. He was saved by Russia's withdrawal of support for the Austrian cause, leading to the Peace of Hubertusburg (1763), which affirmed Prussian ownership of Silesia but saw Saxony freed from its occupation.

Meanwhile, Francis I had worked hard to re-establish Habsburg authority in the empire. Following his coronation, the secular electors and the Wittelsbach elector of Cologne for the first time refused to renew their fiefs and to accord the new emperor the traditional act of homage; many secular princes followed suit. The Bavarian interlude had also forced the Habsburg administration in Vienna to distinguish more clearly than ever before between imperial and Austrian interests. There was overlap, but separate ministers and officials now handled the affairs of the empire and of the Habsburg lands. An Austrian state chancellery (Staatskanzlei) answerable to Maria Theresa existed alongside the imperial chancellery (Reichskanzlei) answerable to Francis I.

In 1746 Francis commissioned a report on whether the empire was actually useful to Austria. Significantly, however, the report clearly concluded that the empire and the Austrian lands needed each other and that it was unthinkable that Austria should relinquish the imperial title.

Francis's greatest achievement was perhaps to rebuild Austrian finances and to create a substantial fortune for what now became the house of Habsburg-Lorraine. He also succeeded in securing the loyalty of the crown's traditional clientele: the bishops, abbots, and other prelates of the imperial church, the imperial cities, and the imperial knights. The hostility of the Wittelsbach elector of Cologne forced Francis to pay close attention to episcopal elections. This laid the foundations for a late revival of Habsburg episcopal politics when his sons came of age and could be candidates for such posts. However, he failed to reform the law courts and both the Reichshofrat and the Reichskammergericht performed poorly during his reign. This led to a growing number of direct appeals to the diet, which created the impression that the empire was unruly and that the emperor was not in control.

Joseph II and the limits of reform

As the spouse of Maria Theresa, Francis I could never enjoy the same prestige as Leopold I or Charles VI. His son Joseph II (r. 1765–90) had better prospects, although he was only joint ruler of the Habsburg lands until Maria Theresa's death in 1780. Nonetheless, the situation in the empire was favourable to the twenty-four-year-old emperor. After the Seven Years War the Prussian king and many other princes were keen to avoid further confrontation, and the confessional animosities of the previous decades cooled.

Shortly before Francis I died the electors themselves had drawn up an imperial reform agenda, which Joseph II extended. Yet he too soon ran into difficulty. Now all the electors and all the 'old princes' (those whose titles were created before about 1550) refused to renew their fiefs. Some minor legislative changes were introduced and he succeeded in defending the imperial knights against Württemberg and Palatinate attempts to annexe their lands, but the princes obstructed anything that they suspected would make the emperor more powerful.

Joseph responded from about 1778 with policies that provoked almost everyone. He wanted to rationalize and modernize the empire but ended up undermining his own authority in it. Displeased with the diet's obstructionism, he connived at paralysing it for over five years. In the scatter of Habsburg lands in southern Germany that were attached to Tyrol he aroused opposition by reforming judicial and administrative structures in ways that infringed the traditional rights of nobles, towns, and rural communities. In the empire generally, he axed all imperial pensions, leaving hundreds of clients embittered. At the same time Joseph reactivated the old right of a newly elected emperor to nominate the first appointment to a prebendaryship in ecclesiastical institutions, to which he invariably appointed his own officials or family members. Finally, his attempts to rationalize episcopal boundaries in the Austrian territories in order to create, in effect, an Austrian Catholic territorial church also alienated many, including his own brother Max Franz, the elector of Cologne.

Joseph's attempts to acquire Bavaria in 1777–9 and 1784 were even more damaging. The idea went back to the 1690s but the fact that the current elector of Bavaria was childless seemed to offer an ideal opportunity. The heir with the strongest claim was Charles Theodore, the elector of the Palatinate, the head of the second Wittelsbach line in the empire, but he had no interest in Bavaria and was willing to do a deal which promised him territory on the Lower Rhine and, ultimately, the Austrian Southern Netherlands. When the Bavarian elector died unexpectedly the deal became public and Prussia declared war at the head of a coalition to protect the empire against Austrian expansionism. Joseph backed down and relinquished all claims to Bavaria in the Treaty of Teschen 1779, which also made Russia, which had brokered the peace, a guarantor of the empire alongside France and Sweden.

In 1784 a second plan apparently covertly supported by Russia—Charles Theodore now even more willing on account of his massive debts—caused such alarm in the empire that the electors of Brandenburg-Prussia, Hanover, and Saxony formed a League of Princes to thwart Joseph, subsequently joined by fourteen further princes, including the elector of Mainz. Once again the project failed and the league faded away, many of its members as worried about falling victim to Prussian ambitions as they were anxious about Joseph's expansionism; by 1788 it was effectively defunct. Just over a year later the emperor was dead. His successor, his brother Leopold II (r. 1790–2), aimed to restore good order, though in the two years of his rule he faced the beginnings of another crisis that was ultimately to destroy the empire.

Older German accounts of the empire in this period argued that the growing confrontation of Brandenburg-Prussia and Austria after 1740 marked the beginning of its end. Both Austria and Prussia allegedly lost interest in the empire and engaged in a struggle for mastery over Germany in which the empire was the victim. The refusal of the princes to renew their fiefs after 1765 is taken as further evidence of indifference among the German ruling elite. The empire did not share the fate of Poland, which ceased to exist in this period following partitions at the hands of Austria, Prussia, and Russia in 1772, 1793, and 1795, but some historians suggest that its ultimate fate in 1806 was similar.

Such arguments reflected the contemptuous view of the empire held by later German historians rather than the indifference of contemporaries. Yet even in the more recent revisionist German histories the narrative of inevitable decline after 1740 persists. In reality, however, interest in the empire remained strong. It is true there was much criticism. Friedrich Carl von Moser spoke for many when he deplored the lack of unity in the 1760s and 1770s and the empire's apparent inability to reform itself. The ecclesiastical territories were subject to growing disparagement by Enlightenment writers who regarded them as anachronisms.

Yet such complaints should be viewed as contributions to a lively reform literature. In the 1760s the young Joseph II inspired many to express their confidence in his ability to renew the empire; his actions in the 1780s prompted many to declare their determination that the empire would survive his recklessness and return to its old historically evolved equilibrium. The anti-imperial propaganda of the League of Princes reiterated all the old themes of Protestant constitutionalism of the 16th and 17th centuries. Vienna responded with a strikingly modern argument: the league's promotion of 'German liberty' was nothing more than a cover for the tyranny of the princes; what the emperor stood for was monarchy founded on popular sovereignty.

Many commentators now wrote about the empire in decidedly modern or Enlightenment terms. They viewed it no longer as a feudal structure but as a federation. In the words of the leading commentator of the late 18th century, the Göttingen scholar Johann Stephan Pütter: it was a 'polity composed of several particular states which, however, still together make a single state'. Pütter clearly articulated the federal view of the empire which characterized the thinking of the League of Princes.

Pütter expressed a patriotism and sense of identification with the empire that was widely shared. Between 1765 and 1790 some 10,000 cases reached the Reichshofrat in Vienna, of which roughly 4,000 involved some 8,000 individuals of modest social origin. In the same period some 7,000 ordinary people were involved in the Reichskammergericht at Wetzlar. The cases came from all over Germany and many of those who appealed to the courts against their own princes described themselves as subjects of the empire, sometimes even as *Reichsbürger* (citizens of the empire). These records convey a strong sense of the rights of subjects in the empire and that many viewed the emperor as their ultimate ruler.

The French Revolution and Napoleon

Much of this was reflected again in the response of German commentators to the French Revolution. For all the enthusiasm that many expressed about events in France there was a widespread conviction that Germany was different. Typical of many was the statement made in 1789 by Freiherr Franz Wilhelm von Spiegel zum Desenberg the administrator of the University of Bonn. The imperial constitution, he declared, was the 'best of all possible forms of government' for 'here the individual has lost less of his natural freedom, less of his political freedom than anywhere else and none of his civil freedom'. The Germans, in other words, did not need to rise up like the French, for they had no need to reclaim something they had never been deprived of in the first place.

This confidence persisted for several years. As late as 1795, the writer Christoph Martin Wieland declared: 'The present constitution of the German Reich, despite its undeniable shortcomings and failings, is on the whole endlessly more conducive to the inner peace and welfare of the nation and more appropriate to its character and to the level of culture upon which it rests.'

Three years previously, however, in April 1792, the new French Republic had declared war on Austria and Prussia. French forces annexed the empire's territories on the left bank of the Rhine, instantly abolishing all feudal rights there, and drove across the Rhine into southern Germany. Despite the problems the empire usually experienced with raising troops, the initial defence effort involving local militias and regional troops was reasonably effective and a force of 200,000 men was agreed by October 1794.

Yet many soon desired peace. In 1795 Brandenburg-Prussia concluded the Peace of Basle with France, which took most of northern Germany out of the conflict and into neutrality until 1806. By 1797 Vienna, after a crushing defeat in Italy, was forced to agree formally to the annexation of the left bank of the Rhine. The estates of the empire followed suit at the Rastatt Congress (1797–9) and the idea gained ground that the ecclesiastical and smaller territories should be used to compensate princes who had lost land and rights to France.

Austria's attempt to reverse the situation by joining the War of the Second Coalition with Britain and Russia in 1799 led to a further defeat and the confirmation of the French annexations at the Peace of Lunéville in 1801. When Francis II refused to preside over a conference to reorganize the empire, the diet had no option but to proceed; indeed princes who had lost lands engaged in the process with some enthusiasm.

In 1803 the Reichsdeputationshauptschluss proposed a radical restructuring of the empire. The cession of the left bank of the

8. Francis II's rule was terminated by Napoleon's ultimatum; two years previously he had already assumed the title of Emperor Francis I.

Rhine to France was confirmed; on the right bank three electorates, nineteen bishoprics, forty-four abbeys, almost all of the imperial cities, and all the lands of the imperial knights disappeared; in all about 10,000 square kilometres of land and some three million people were incorporated into new territories. The major winners were Brandenburg-Prussia (in the Rhineland), Baden, Württemberg, and Bavaria. The disappearance of the ecclesiastical territories gave the Protestant princes a majority for the first time, which threatened the Habsburgs' position in the empire. Because the ecclesiastical electorates were abolished, four new electorates were created for Baden, Hesse-Kassel, Salzburg, and Württemberg.

French pressure on the empire remained relentless. In 1804 Francis II (see Figure 8) assumed the title of emperor of Austria (as Francis I), largely to pre-empt Napoleon's formal adoption of an imperial title in the same year. Following another disastrous Austrian defeat and a humiliating peace at Pressburg in December 1805, Napoleon also recognized the full sovereignty of Bavaria and Württemberg as kingdoms and of Baden and Hesse-Darmstadt as grand duchies. Sixteen German princes in southern and western Germany now abandoned the empire by joining the French-dominated Confederation of the Rhine. On 1 August 1806 Napoleon sent a message to the diet saying that he regarded the empire as defunct and threatened the emperor with another occupation of Austria if he did not relinquish the imperial throne. Francis II then agreed to abdicate. The formal announcement of the empire's dissolution on 6 August 1806 released all German rulers from their obligations to him because the empire had already ceased to exist. A thousand-year history had come to an end.

Epilogue: the legacy of the Holy Roman Empire

After 1806

Histories of Germany written before 1945 usually asserted that the Holy Roman Empire had disappeared in 1806 without so much as a murmur and that it left virtually no trace in German history. In fact there is much evidence that its demise generated shock and disbelief. There also seems to have been widespread nostalgia for it. Yet such sentiments were undoubtedly overshadowed by the rapid pace of events and the larger questions that dominated between 1806 and 1815.

Secularization of the imperial church lands and mediatization of the numerous smaller territories resulted in the enlargement of those that remained which also became sovereign states for the first time. Napoleon created a new kingdom in Westphalia for his brother Jerome; he also made Bavaria and Württemberg into kingdoms and Baden and Hesse-Darmstadt into grand duchies, all tied to France in the new Confederation of the Rhine. This was designed to isolate Prussia in the north-east and Austria in the south-east. Further territorial changes occurred subsequently, and much of Westphalia was given to Prussia in 1815, so that only thirty-nine states were left to join the German Confederation in 1815.

This whole process, in which some former rulers became subjects for the first time and millions acquired new rulers, sometimes more than once, was accompanied by a debate about the larger framework within which Germans lived. The dissolution of the empire in 1806 effectively partitioned its territory into four zones: the areas directly occupied by France, the French-dominated Confederation of the Rhine, Prussia, and Austria. That immediately raised the question of whether 'Germany' would ever be united again. Some looked forward to the restoration of the Holy Roman Empire. Others advocated an Austrian–Prussian condominium in which the two spheres of influence would be divided by the River Main. A third option also soon gathered ground: some kind of federation that would both preserve the sovereign states and guarantee some kind of common bond.

Alongside these concrete discussions young Romantic writers avowed their faith in the greatness of the medieval empire and propagated ideas of a new empire in the future. Young patriots, often described as the first real German nationalists, envisaged a reunification of Germany that would unite all Germans and eliminate the princes whose selfish behaviour they blamed for their present plight. Figures such as Johann Gottlieb Fichte, Friedrich Ludwig Jahn, and Ernst Moritz Arndt have often been seen as the first prophets of a new and dangerous form of German nationalism. Their immediate main wishes were that the French should be expelled, that German unity should be restored, and that power should be given to the German people. The fiery nationalism and anti-French rhetoric of these writers made them useful to the Prussian government in the final war against Napoleon which began in 1813. On the other hand their republicanism and democratic convictions made them suspect as soon as the war had been won.

The actual significance of the Romantic writers and patriotic volunteers in the struggle against Napoleon has often been overestimated. The war was won by Russian, Austrian, and Prussian troops and the future of 'Germany' was decided by those who championed the interests of the sovereign states. Bavaria had left the Confederation of the Rhine just before the battle of Leipzig in October 1813. Württemberg, Baden, Hesse-Darmstadt, and Hesse-Kassel left just after.

The plans of Freiherr vom Stein and his secretary Arndt for a strong German national imperial state, influenced by both Romantic and patriotic visions, ultimately served only as a useful foil in the complex negotiations over the future of the German lands which were dominated by the Prussian chancellor Karl August von Hardenberg and the Austrian foreign minister Klemens von Metternich.

Both were at root, though for different reasons, sceptics on the 'national' issue. Hardenberg had great nostalgia for the old empire as the system which had united Germans for a thousand years, but he recognized that the creation of the new sovereign German states could not be undone. Metternich was less sentimental and rapidly concluded that the Holy Roman Empire under Austrian leadership had no future. Himself the scion of a dynasty of imperial knights, originally nobles in the electorate of Trier, which had lost its lands in the French occupation of the Rhineland and the subsequent secularization and mediatization, Metternich sold the lands his father received as compensation. He retained ownership of Schloss Johannisberg in the Rheingau, his reward from Francis I for his services in securing Austria's victory over Napoleon and for representing Austria's interests at the Congress of Vienna, but he made Plasy in Bohemia the new residence for his family. For Metternich the creation of the German Confederation with Austria as its presiding power was the logical outcome of the assumption of the new Austrian imperial title in 1804 and the dissolution of the Holy Roman Empire in 1806.

The German Confederation and after

The new sovereign states were determined to hold on to their status and their authority over their newly acquired lands and subjects. Yet the German Confederation guaranteed elements of continuity. Its frontiers were the same as those of the old empire; the eastern provinces of Prussia (East and West Prussia and Posen) were only included after 1848. As in the old empire, the diet of the Confederation included only representatives of the rulers not of the people, though this was increasingly criticized. The articles of confederation also sought to secure for the future the rights that Germans had enjoyed in the past: the right of Germans to representation, freedom of mobility, property rights, the liberty of the three main Christian confessions, and the equality in civil and political rights of their members along with the promise of a law concerning freedom of the press.

The Confederation was a league of states rather than a federation or confederation, but it contained enough familiar elements to justify claims that the Confederation was in essence a continuation of the old empire. On the other hand there was growing criticism of the inadequacy of its defence capability, of the lack of progress in defining citizens' rights, of the absence of the kind of supra-territorial supreme court that had existed in the old empire, and, reflecting newer concerns, of the fact that there was no central representative body. This discontent was one of the causes of the 1848 revolutions in Germany, but the Frankfurt Parliament failed to bring about change.

The growing preoccupation with greater unity as the answer to the inadequacies of the Confederation after the failure of the Frankfurt Parliament, the revival of Romantic ideas about a strong empire, and the renewed confidence and ambition of Prussian policies in Germany led to the Austro-Prussian war in 1866 and the creation of the German empire in 1871. That empire excluded Austria and this marked a new departure in German history. Its federal nature, however, again reflected the pattern established under the old empire. But while the new Hohenzollern emperors were pleased to invoke the medieval Hohenstaufen emperors when it suited them, the new empire in reality had little to do with the old.

Ideas of a greater Germany gained currency again in the 1920s after the failure of both the Hohenzollern and Habsburg empires. The penalties imposed on Germany and Austria in 1918–19, in particular the territorial losses, led many to think that a union of the German Austrian republics might be timely, but that was promptly prohibited by the victorious powers. Hitler's plans for a greater German empire on the one hand rejected previous German history as worthless, but on the other hand claimed to fulfil Germany's destiny. Hitler underlined this as early as 1934 by replacing Germany's traditional federal structure with the Nazi party regional organization.

Perceptions of the empire since 1945

The end of the Third Reich did not immediately change attitudes. In the German Democratic Republic, the old empire was viewed as a doomed feudal society with no relevance to the present. In the Federal Republic of Germany there was a slow revival of interest. Catholic historians were interested in the old empire as a benign alternative to the disastrous Prussian-dominated Protestant empire. Its corporatist society also made it attractive to those who sought strong societal structures reinforced by Christianity as a bulwark against both a revival of Nazism and the spread of communism.

Above all, the history of the old empire fitted in well with the emerging narrative of the new Federal Republic as a post-national, pro-European state. From the 1950s West German historians such as Heinrich Lutz, Konrad Repgen, and Karl Otmar von Aretin laid the foundations for a new view of the early modern empire. Since then more historical research has been done on the empire than ever before. Yet it seems to have had little wider resonance. Despite the success of major exhibitions in Magdeburg and Berlin marking the second centenary of the empire's dissolution in 2006, it is difficult to see much evidence that the empire still has any real meaning for the German public or that even vague knowledge of it is widely present.

The situation in Austria is little different. Here there was a radical turn away from the common German past after 1945, and the scholarly revival of interest in the Holy Roman Empire both came later than in the Federal Republic and has been more limited. The writing of Austrian history still downplays the significance of the empire for the development of Austria as a great power. For both Austrians and Germans even the word *Reich* was utterly discredited after 1945.

How seriously, therefore, can one take the invocation of the old empire in contemporary metanarratives, in particular the narrative of Europe with a post-national Germany at its centre? How valid are the arguments about its relevance as a model for the present? Can the old German empire really serve as a model for Europe?

The old empire belongs to the past and cannot be revived. On the other hand, there is no doubt that its traditions of law and of rights contributed, alongside the traditions that evolved in other European countries, to the development of modern Europe. In view of the prevalence of claims in German historiography which have so often denied the contributions made by German society to Western notions of democracy and freedom, even that is an important insight.

It seems inevitable that, in one way or another, with or without popular resonance, the old empire will live on in the narratives constructed by historians and others. If the European Union survives its current crisis, the arguments about parallels may become more popular again. If the European Union fails, one could imagine another set of comparisons being made, seeing the failure of the EU pre-shadowed by the failure of the Holy Roman Empire. Historical narratives are invariably shaped by present events.

Nothing can detract, however, from the empire's very real achievements. Its multi-level system of government laid the foundations for an enduring federal system and for the rich regional and cultural variety that developed with it. The multitude of court and urban centres, the ambitions of princes, and the pride of free cities generated extensive patronage in all forms of cultural production.

From an early stage the empire functioned as a peacekeeping system for the centre of Europe and, despite tensions, it developed conflict resolution mechanisms that enabled the small territories to survive alongside the large ones. It was not free of internal conflicts or of civil wars but the restoration of unity was the invariable outcome. It proceeded on the basis of negotiation and compromise rather than violence and civil war. It developed remarkable common legal institutions and an extensive body of law which protected the subjects of the empire. Alongside Switzerland, it was the only European polity which devised a satisfactory lasting solution to the religious divide of the 16th century.

The empire far exceeded the lifespan of any subsequent German state; from that point of view it remains the most successful polity in German history. Above all it provided the framework within which the German language and German identity developed over a thousand years. The Holy Roman Empire, which began as a Frankish kingdom, ended as a truly German empire.

Chronology

3rd century AD	Frankish tribes, including Germanic groups, attack the Roman Empire; some settle and intermarry with the provincial Roman elites.
324	Constantine founded a new capital at Byzantium (renamed Constantinople); the aim to restore the entire Roman Empire failed.
395	Division of the Roman Empire into a western and an eastern empire.
476	The last western Roman emperor, Augustulus, was deposed by the leader of the Goths.
481	Clovis of the Frankish Merovingian dynasty became king of the Franks.
534	The eastern emperor Justinian I issued his *corpus juris civilis*, a code of civil law intended for the whole Roman empire, though he controlled very little of its western parts.
751	The Merovingian kings deposed by the Pepinid dynasty, later known as Carolingians.
800	Charlemagne, the sole Pepinid ruler of the Franks since 711, crowned emperor in Rome by Pope Leo III on Christmas Day.
840–3	Charlemagne's empire divided into three kingdoms.
880	The Treaty of Ribemont established the frontier between the western and the eastern Frankish kingdoms.
911	Extinction of the East Frankish Carolingian line on the death of Louis the Child.

911–18	Duke Conrad I of Franconia elected king but died childless.
919	Henry, duke of Saxony, elected king; his successors in the Ottonian dynasty rule until 1024.
936–73	Otto I 'the Great' once more united the German crown with the imperial crown from 962.
1024	The Ottonian line became extinct with the death of Henry II. The election of Conrad II of Franconia inaugurated the rule of the Salians until 1138.
1033	Conrad II crowned king of Burgundy, bringing it into the empire following the death of the last ruler of the Rudolfine dynasty which had ruled since 888.
1075	Start of the Investiture Contest.
1122	The Concordat of Worms ended the Investiture Contest.
1125	Following the death of Henry V, Lothair of Supplinburg elected as king.
1138	The Staufer Conrad III had successfully asserted his claims to rule and inaugurated the period of Staufer rule until 1250.
1152	Accession of Conrad's nephew Frederick I 'Barbarossa'.
1190–7	Henry VI elected king; he also inherited the Sicilian throne, but died after only six years on the throne.
1215	Henry's son, Frederick II, crowned in Aachen and devoted his reign to establishing Staufer authority in Italy. His reign ended in failure in 1250.
1250–73	The era of the 'lesser kings' (to 1347) began with the Interregnum characterized by a succession of weak rulers, none of whom became emperors.
1273–91	Rudolf of Habsburg sought to re-impose imperial authority but was unable to establish his dynasty.
1315	Henry VII was the first king since Frederick II to be crowned emperor but his death the following year led to another double election.
1338	The era of 'lesser kings' saw the emergence of a small group of leading nobles who declared themselves at a meeting in Rhens to be the sole legitimate electors.
1347–78	Charles IV, Henry VII's grandson, ruled the empire from Prague, which became an archbishopric and the seat of the first 'German' university in 1348.

1356	The Golden Bull confirmed the archbishops of Mainz, Cologne, and Trier, and the king of Bohemia, the count Palatine, and the dukes of Saxony and Brandenburg as electors to the German crown.
1378–1400	Charles IV's heir Wenceslas was unable to survive as emperor.
1400–10	Rupert of the Palatinate lacked a power base comparable to Bohemia.
1410–37	Charles IV's second son Sigismund (crowned emperor 1433) resolved the problems of the papacy at the Council of Constance 1414–18.
1438–9	Sigismund succeeded by his son-in-law Albert II of Austria, whose own son, born after his death, could not be elected king in Germany.
1440–93	Election of Frederick III, Albert II's cousin, initiated continuous Habsburg rule in the empire.
1493–1519	Maximilian I inherited both the Austrian lands and the duchy of Burgundy; he also had ambitions of regaining Italy and of reforming the empire.
1495	Reform Diet or Reichstag at Worms.
1517	Martin Luther's public protest in Wittenberg against the sale of indulgences marked the start of the Reformation.
1519–56	Charles V, Maximilian I's grandson, succeeded as emperor in addition to being king of Spain. In 1530, he became the last Holy Roman Emperor to be crowned by the pope.
1521	At the diet of Worms, Charles outlawed Luther but the elector of Saxony refused to recognize the emperor's authority to arrest one of his subjects.
1525	The Peasants' War prompted many princes to take control over the religious reform movement in their territories.
1531	The Schmalkaldic League was formed to protect the interests of the Protestant princes and cities.
1546–7	Charles V attempted to crush Protestantism in Germany by military intervention and to impose Catholicism on the empire. By 1552 he had failed.
1555	The religious Peace of Augsburg recognized the rights of Protestants in which formally became a bi-confessional polity; the fundamental principle was that of *cuius regio, eius religio* (the religion of a ruler should dictate the religion of a territory).

1556	Charles V abdicated: his Spanish lands went to his son Philip (II of Spain); his German lands and the imperial title went to his brother Ferdinand.
1556–76	Both Ferdinand I (r. 1556–64) and Maximilian II (r. 1564–76) ruled within the framework established around 1500, the reforms of the reign of Maximilian I, and by the Peace of Augsburg in 1555.
1576–1612	Under Rudolf II, especially from about 1600, the empire experienced growing internal tensions, many arising from questions about the religious peace.
1612–19	Emperor Matthias ruled in the conciliatory style of Ferdinand I and Maximilian II.
1617	The election of Ferdinand of Styria as heir to the Bohemian throne precipitated the Thirty Years War.
1618–48	Thirty Years War.
1618	The Bohemian Protestant nobles in 1618 deposed Ferdinand; election of the Calvinist elector of the Palatinate as king.
1619	As emperor, Ferdinand fought to regain Bohemia and control Germany.
1648	The Treaty of Osnabrück, part of the Peace of Westphalia, reverted to the constitutional balance between emperor and estates that had been articulated around 1500 and reiterated in the Peace of Augsburg 1555.
1637–57	Ferdinand III ended the conflict started by his father Ferdinand II and managed the early years of the peace.
1658–1705	Leopold I re-established imperial authority.
1658–68	Anti-Habsburg League of the Rhine.
1663	Imperial diet or Reichstag opens and remains in permanent session to 1806.
1672–8	French war against the Netherlands.
1674–7	French attack on Lorraine and Alsace.
1679	Peace of Nijmegen between France and the empire.
1679–84	French annexations (*Réunions*) of western territories of the empire, including Strasbourg 1681.
1683	Ottoman siege of Vienna.
1692	Creation of the Electorate of Hanover.

1697	Election of the Elector of Saxony as king of Poland.
1699	Peace of Carlowitz with the Ottoman Empire.
1700–21	Great Northern War.
1701	Coronation of the Elector of Brandenburg as king in Prussia.
1701–14	War of the Spanish Succession, ended by Peace of Rastatt.
1705–11	Joseph I.
1711–40	Charles IV.
1713	Pragmatic Sanction: Maria Theresa to be recognized as heir to the Habsburg lands but not to the German crown.
1716–18	Turkish war, ended by Peace of Passarowitz.
1732	Pragmatic Sanction confirmed by the empire.
1733–5	War of the Polish Succession.
1740–2	Interregnum following the death of Charles VI; his daughter Maria Theresa inherited the Habsburg lands.
1740–2	Frederick II seized Silesia from Austria (First Silesian War).
1742	Election of Charles Albert of Bavaria as Emperor Charles VII.
1744–5	Second Silesian War.
1745	Election of Francis Stephen of Lorraine as Emperor Francis I.
1756–63	Seven Years War (Third Silesian War).
1765–90	Joseph II.
1767–8	Attempted reform of the Reichskammergericht.
1772	First Partition of Poland.
1778–9	War of the Bavarian Succession, ended by Peace of Teschen.
1780	Joseph II sole ruler of the Habsburg lands after the death of Maria Theresa.
1785	A League of Princes, strongly supported by Brandenburg-Prussia, thwarted Joseph II's second attempt to acquire Bavaria.
1789	Revolution in France.
1790–2	Leopold II.
1792–7	French declaration of war against Austria and Prussia.

1792–1806	Francis II.
1795	Peace of Basle: Prussia made peace with France, leaving Austria to fight on.
1797	Peace of Campo Formio: France forced Austria to accept de facto the annexation of the left bank of the Rhine.
1797–9	Rastatt Congress: the empire considered the implications of the French occupation of the left bank of the Rhine.
1801	Peace of Lunéville: Austria and the empire forced to accept the French annexation of the left bank of the Rhine *de jure*.
1803	Reichsdeputationshauptschluss: the Reichstag agreed to compensate princes who had lost lands on the left bank of the Rhine by dissolving the ecclesiastical territories and by turning most imperial cities into territorial towns.
1804	Francis II assumed the title of emperor of Austria (as Francis I) in anticipation of Napoleon's assumption of the title of emperor of France.
1806	Napoleon elevated Bavaria and Württemberg into kingdoms and formed the Confederation of the Rhine. In response to an ultimatum from Napoleon, Francis II agreed to dissolve the Holy Roman Empire.

Further reading

Abulafia, D. S. A., *Frederick II: A Medieval Emperor* (London, 1988).

Althoff, Gerd, *Otto III*, transl. Phyllis G. Jestice (Philadelphia, PA, 2003).

Arnold, Benjamin, *Medieval Germany, 500–1300: A Political Interpretation* (Toronto, 1997).

Blanning, T. C. W., *The French Revolution in Germany: Occupation and Resistance in the Rhineland 1791–1802* (Oxford, 1983).

Blanning, Tim, *The Culture of Power and the Power of Culture: Old Regime Europe 1660–1789* (Oxford, 2002).

Blanning, Tim, 'The Holy Roman Empire of the German Nation Past and Present', *Historical Research*, 85 (2012), 57–70.

Blanning, Tim, *Frederick the Great: King of Prussia* (London, 2015).

Brady, Thomas A., *German Histories in the Age of Reformations, 1400–1650* (Cambridge, 2009).

Clark, Christopher, *Iron Kingdom: The Rise and Downfall of Prussia, 1600–1947* (London, 2006).

Coy, Jason Phillip et al., *The Holy Roman Empire, Reconsidered* (New York, 2010).

Du Boulay, F. R. H., *Germany in the Later Middle Ages* (London, 1983).

Fichtner, Paula Sutter, *Emperor Maximilian II* (New Haven, CT, 2001).

Fichtner, Paula Sutter, *Terror and Toleration: The Habsburg Empire Confronts Islam, 1526–1850* (Chicago, 2008).

Forster, Marc R., *Catholic Germany from the Reformation to the Enlightenment* (Houndmills, 2007).

Freed, John, *Frederick Barbarossa: The Prince and the Myth* (New Haven, CT, 2016).

Friedeburg, Robert von, *Luther's Legacy: The Thirty Years War and the Modern Notion of 'State' in the Empire, 1530s to 1790s* (Cambridge, 2016).

Fuchs, R.-P. 'The Supreme Court of the Holy Roman Empire', *The Sixteenth-Century Journal*, 34 (2003), 9–27.

Fuhrmann, Horst, *Germany in the High Middle Ages, c.1050–1200* (Cambridge, 1986).

Gagliardo, John G., *Reich and Nation: The Holy Roman Empire as Idea and Reality, 1763–1806* (Bloomington, IN, 1980).

Gross, Hanns, *Empire and Sovereignty: A History of German Public Law in the Holy Roman Empire, 1599–1804* (Chicago, 1973).

Haverkamp, Alfred, *Medieval Germany, 1056–1273*, transl. R. Mortimer and H. Braun (Oxford, 1988).

Heal, Bridget, *The Cult of the Virgin Mary in Early Modern Germany: Protestant and Catholic Piety, 1500–1648* (Cambridge, 2007).

Heal, Bridget, *A Magnificent Faith: Art and Identity in Lutheran Germany* (Oxford, 2017).

Herwig, Wolfram, *Conrad II, 990–1039: Emperor of Three Kingdoms*, transl. Denise A. Kaiser (Philadelphia, PA, 2006).

Hirschi, Caspar, *The Origins of Nationalism: An Alternative History from Ancient Rome to Early Modern Germany* (Cambridge, 2011).

Hughes, Michael, *Law and Politics in Eighteenth-Century Germany: The Imperial Aulic Council in the Reign of Charles VI* (Woodbridge, 1988).

Leyser, Karl, *Medieval Germany and its Neighbours, 900–1250* (London, 1982).

McKitterick, Rosamond, *Charlemagne: The Formation of a European Identity* (Cambridge, 2008).

The New Cambridge Medieval History, 7 vols, various eds (Cambridge, 1995–2005).

Nicholas, David, *The Northern Lands: Germanic Europe, c. 1270–c. 1500* (Oxford, 2009).

Pursell, Brennan C., *The Winter King: Frederick V of the Palatinate and the Coming of the Thirty Years War* (Aldershot, 2003).

Reuter, Timothy, *Germany in the Early Middle Ages, c. 800–1056* (London, 1991).

Robinson, Ian S., *Henry IV of Germany* (Cambridge, 2000).

Rublack, Ulinka, *Reformation Europe* (Cambridge, 2005).

Scales, Len, 'Late Medieval Germany: An Under-Stated Nation?', in Len Scales and Oliver Zimmer, eds, *Power and the Nation in European History* (Cambridge, 2005), 166–91.

Scales, Len, *The Shaping of German Identity: Authority and Crisis, 1245-1414* (Cambridge, 2012).

Scott, Tom, *Society and Economy in Germany, 1300-1600* (Houndmills, 2002).

Scott Dixon, C., *The German Reformation* (Oxford, 2002).

Scott Dixon, C., *Contesting the Reformation* (Oxford, 2012).

Stollberg-Rilinger, Barbara, *The Emperor's Old Clothes: Constitutional History and the Symbolic Language of the Holy Roman Empire*, transl. Thomas Dunlap (New York, 2015).

Todd, Malcolm, *The Early Germans*, 2nd edn (Oxford, 2004).

Weinfurter, Stefan, *The Salian Century: Main Currents in an Age of Transition*, transl. Barbara M. Bowlus (Philadelphia, PA, 1999).

Whaley, Joachim, 'Thinking about Germany, 1750-1815: The Birth of a Nation?', *Publications of the English Goethe Society*, NS 66 (1996), 53-72.

Whaley, Joachim, 'The Old Reich in Modern Memory: Recent Controversies Concerning the "Relevance" of Early Modern German History', in David Midgley and Christian Emden, eds, *German History, Literature and the Nation (Selected Papers from the Conference 'The Fragile Tradition', Cambridge 2002, vol. 2)* (Oxford, 2004), 25-49.

Whaley, Joachim, '*Reich, Nation, Volk*: Early Modern Perspectives', *Modern Language Review*, 101 (2006), 442-55.

Whaley, Joachim, 'The Transformation of the Aufklärung: From the Idea of Power to the Power of Ideas', in H. M. Scott and B. Simms, eds, *Cultures of Power* (Cambridge, 2007), 158-79.

Whaley, Joachim, 'A German Nation? National and Confessional Identities Before the Thirty Years War', in R. J. W. Evans, Michael Schaich, and Peter H. Wilson, eds, *The Holy Roman Empire 1495-1806* (Oxford, 2011), 303-21.

Whaley, Joachim, *Germany and the Holy Roman Empire, 1493-1806*, 2 vols (Oxford, 2012).

Whaley, Joachim, 'Hier existiert noch das alte heilige deutsche Reich: The Legacy of the Holy Roman Empire and the Unity of Germany', *Publications of the English Goethe Society*, 83 (2014), 1-21.

Whaley, Joachim, 'Wahre Aufklärung kann erreicht und segensreich werden: The German Enlightenment and its Interpretation', *Oxford German Studies*, 44 (2015), 428-48.

Wilson, Peter H., *From Reich to Revolution: German History 1558-1806* (Basingstoke, 2004).

Wilson, Peter H., 'Still a Monstrosity? Some Reflections on Early Modern German Statehood', *The Historical Journal*, 49 (2006), 565–76.

Wilson, Peter H., 'Prussia's Relations with the Holy Roman Empire, 1740–1786', *The Historical Journal*, 51 (2008), 337–71.

Wilson, Peter H., *Europe's Tragedy: A History of the Thirty Years War* (London, 2009).

Wilson, Peter H., *The Holy Roman Empire: A Thousand Years of Europe's History* (London, 2016).

Index

Z

SOCIAL MEDIA
Very Short Introduction

Join our community
www.oup.com/vsi

- Join us online at the official Very Short Introductions **Facebook** page.
- Access the thoughts and musings of our authors with our online **blog**.
- Sign up for our monthly **e-newsletter** to receive information on all new titles publishing that month.
- Browse the full range of Very Short Introductions online.
- Read **extracts** from the Introductions for free.
- If you are a teacher or lecturer you can order inspection copies quickly and simply via our website.

AFRICAN HISTORY
A Very Short Introduction
John Parker & Richard Rathbone

Essential reading for anyone interested in the African continent
and the diversity of human history, this *Very Short Introduction*
looks at Africa's past and reflects on the changing ways it has
been imagined and represented. Key themes in current thinking
about Africa's history are illustrated with a range of fascinating
historical examples, drawn from over 5 millennia across this
vast continent.

'A very well informed and sharply stated historiography... should
be in every historiography student's kitbag. A tour de force... it
made me think a great deal.'

Terence Ranger,
The Bulletin of the School of Oriental and African Studies

www.oup.com/vsi

GERMAN LITERATURE
A Very Short Introduction
Nicholas Boyle

German writers, from Luther and Goethe to Heine, Brecht,
and Günter Grass, have had a profound influence on the modern
world. This *Very Short Introduction* presents an engrossing tour
of the course of German literature from the late Middle Ages to
the present, focussing especially on the last 250 years.
Emphasizing the economic and religious context of many
masterpieces of German literature, it highlights how they can be
interpreted as responses to social and political changes within
an often violent and tragic history. The result is a new and clear
perspective which illuminates the power of German literature
and the German intellectual tradition, and its impact on the
wider cultural world.

> 'Boyle has a sure touch and an obvious authority...this is a
> balanced and lively introduction to German literature.'
>
> Ben Hutchinson, TLS

GERMAN
PHILOSOPHY
A Very Short Introduction
Andrew Bowie

German Philosophy: A Very Short Introduction discusses the idea that German philosophy forms one of the most revealing responses to the problems of 'modernity'. The rise of the modern natural sciences and the related decline of religion raises a series of questions, which recur throughout German philosophy, concerning the relationships between knowledge and faith, reason and emotion, and scientific, ethical, and artistic ways of seeing the world. There are also many significant philosophers who are generally neglected in most existing English-language treatments of German philosophy, which tend to concentrate on the canonical figures. This *Very Short Introduction* will include reference to these thinkers and suggests how they can be used to question more familiar German philosophical thought.

www.oup.com/vsi